THE ASCENSION PERSPECTIVE

HOW TO RISE ABOVE THE CHAOS OF LIFE

Collected and edited by

Dr. Kelly Randolph Bennett
and
Charlie Romney-Brown, M.A.

THOMAS NOBLE
BOOKS

THOMAS NOBLE BOOKS

Thomas Noble Books

Wilmington, DE

www.thomasnoblebooks.com

ISBN: 9781945586064

Library of Congress Control Number: 2017946419

Printed in the United States of America

First Printing 2017

Cover design by Sarah Barrie of Cyanotype.ca

Editing by Gwen Hoffnagle

TABLE OF CONTENTS

PROLOGUE

The Ascension Perspective tells you what you always wanted to know about this journey called life and what really matters in the long run. If you are preoccupied with concerns such as "How do I prepare for what might happen?" or "I feel powerless to prevent the destruction of this planet" or even "Does my life count for anything beyond the obvious?" this book is for you!

The Ascension Perspective clarifies what is worth caring about on a daily basis as well as what ultimately counts! All is viewed from the standpoint of the whole of creation, a universal perspective. It reflects a sweeping outlook on the potential impact of what really matters to life on Planet Earth.

Consider that a dramatic transformation of life here is inevitable and not just a virtual event. And when it takes place, what will be the profound implications? This book tells of important themes on which to focus in preparing for an imminent Planetary Transformation that involves everyone and every living thing, the effects of which will reverberate throughout the Cosmos. With such a far-reaching outlook, *The Ascension Perspective* will become your trustworthy guidebook for creating a picture of what Planetary Transformation requires, what it involves, how it is to be done, and how to find your unique role in it. Even better, it prepares you for attaining the incredible prize of Ascension, which is available to everyone on Earth!

Complementary to all religious and spiritual orientations, this new gospel of LIFE is revealed for all mankind – a collection of modernized principles intended for living a

joyous, complete, and secure life. These principles apply across cultural and individual differences and are suited for twenty-first century living and beyond. They are capable of creating new perspectives, new skills, and new purpose within each one of us. With this knowledge you can create your own true channel of communication with your higher power, direct and free of misleading distortions.

In addition, by applying these new principles to your life you can divest yourself of the powerful influences that have controlled your evolution! Consequently the slow-moving evolutionary pace that you have sustained until now will speed up, reducing significantly the evolutionary gap that keeps you from becoming the person you yearn to be. *The Ascension Perspective* shows you how to access complete healing and renewal, including that of your DNA. Amazing!

* * *

How did I stumble across such vital information? My source of evolutionary wisdom is the art of meditation, and it has been a reliable source of profound wisdom since I was formally introduced to it in the early 1970s. From childhood I have followed directions from my intuition and sensed the related energy shifts in my body that I could not ignore. Once introduced to meditation, I searched for ways to learn about myself and my relationship to life. Much of the time I didn't know what I was doing. I relied entirely on the receptiveness of others who gave me information about how to guide my life. I trusted others' devotion, skills, and care, applying whatever truth I could recognize. Often the messages were meaningful, while at other times not at all. Sometimes they were direct and clear; other times symbolic or vague. Seeking wisdom through others' eyes was productive only to a point, and not completely satisfying.

Then one day things radically changed! Beginning in early 2002, a mass of principles of living and personal instructions presented themselves during formal meditations. Because there was unusual clarity, with a distinct ring of truth, I felt the information was credible and recorded everything for 15 years – thousands of hours of conversations. The impact of these conversations on my life has been profound.

Early in this recording effort, and more than a year before publishing my first book, *Too Much Too Little Just Right*, in 2003, I was informed that there would be a second book to be written jointly with **my source, who was introduced as LIFE Itself, Father Creator, or God who speaks with multiple voices. (To minimize confusion, I combined all these titles for God into the word *LIFE*.)**

We are progressing rapidly beyond words. Your next book will help people know what to care about from seeing an expanded picture, even a universal perspective. It would be useful to start writing it now, once again with Our inspiration. In other words, We will write it with you.

"Thank You. I would like that very much."

Then We will. The book's content will present, from Our perspective, what really matters in living life on this planet while caring about issues that truly count in the end. The book will articulate universal perspectives and their potential impact on Planet Earth and all who live here.

"Are You talking about defining universal principles?

Yes. We mean universal principles as applied to the context of Earth.

"Will the writing of the next book be a role that my wife, Charlie, and I will play in the bigger picture?"

Writing the book will prepare you to articulate what is important enough to be said, and at the same time will prepare people for a larger set of principles by which to live a life of wholeness with the joy We offer.

As described in your first book, seeing the whole picture permits a person to find the best solution to any problem and the best path for their life. However, to do this a person's perspective must expand.

You can live in either a limited or expanded mode. While the latter is more inclusive, both are real. We accept both, but yearn for the more expanded perspective, which includes all possibilities. Your roles are to help others include all possibilities.

A four-dimensional Earth experience is not enough for bringing universal principles to everyday life. In order to portray Our transforming power, you must be able to see the whole picture as We do. All possibilities must be in the picture for wholeness. We said that We would write the books with you, didn't We? This ensures that Our energy permeates the writings, making transformation a real, not a virtual event.

"What do you mean by the word *transformation?*"

When We speak of Planetary Transformation, We are talking about a major change in worldwide consciousness, even unbelievable change in some cases. For the planet to be transformed, everyone must be involved. Everyone will be affected in some way, with some more changed than others, but no one will remain unmoved by the message.

With modern communications it is now possible to reach everybody on the planet to some degree. The power of the message will carry it into the most remote places. Those most influenced by it will make the greatest contributions to this complete change and will get the most return for their efforts.

* * *

"Please comment on the structure of the new book or books. Are we moving in the right direction?"

Yes, so far so good. Keep it fluid for any changes that occur. We will be the guiding nudge. You will become aware of the changes as you go along.

Remain open to nuances and meanings of principles that deserve attention. We are interested in principles that guide people's lives on a daily basis. Our focus is on the clarity of the principles and their widespread application, separate from culture and individual differences.

There is a common thread that runs through humanity everywhere, composed of strands of principles that can be derived from one's daily experience. To define a principle takes an ability to distill it from experiences. We want humankind to be better prepared to do this, along with having an awareness of Our *energy presence*. By asking, "What does this experience mean toward a principle for living?" the reader brings curiosity into the equation. **A foremost reason for this book's existence is to assist its reader to find and use these principles of living.**

Our message to the world through you will be "published" in many ways. We use the word *proclamations* because what We have to say will be "official," from LIFE. It will be news to the reader, a new gospel of living, helpful to all. You will be the vehicle for this publication or proclamation.

You will get the word directly this way, undistorted by outside noise. This lack of noise will give the proclamations veracity overall. For a change, Our voice will be heard undistorted. **Before long, people will have their own channels of communication, as you and Charlie do, with connections linked directly to LIFE.**

* * *

"Something is happening today! I am feeling a change take place… perhaps it's an ability to look at things differently."

Not surprising! It is a new perspective that We are masterful at supplying to those who can receive it. The very questions you ask provide Our access to this kind of change, because questions open the door for Us to operate. We want to be available to you.

The significance of a team effort becomes apparent. Accomplishment of our goals cannot occur without it. For success, we truly need each other interdependently.

* * *

"I have questions from reading a spiritually oriented magazine yesterday. All kinds of gurus, sages, and pundits are portrayed and advertised in the magazine. Are Charlie and I going to be two of the bunch? Are we to respect or ignore what the gurus are doing?

Nothing happens in your lives now without Our influence. Nothing! In the magazine you were exposed to a smattering of approaches to LIFE that the world has available for application. Since every person is different from another, We need to offer many approaches, providing opportunities for everyone to find Us. Although the gurus' messages are somewhat dissimilar, their goals are the same: unity with Us. We need someone to influence all of these "tributaries" to merge their teachings into one major stream that will bring about Planetary Transformation.

We are giving you and Charlie a unifying message. The proclamations, in whatever form they take, will combine these many approaches into a major force that will turn the world around. Hence Planetary Transformation! So respect and ignore those pundits for the time being and focus on the unifying message that We supply through conversations with you.

What you receive will astound you when you begin to formulate the final product. Do not underestimate the power of what you are doing to contribute to Planetary Transformation. You are essential pieces in the jigsaw puzzle of Our plan. Your book will describe how to fit the pieces together to make the picture that Planetary Transformation requires.

As Our message, LIFE is introducing a new idea that can become a worldwide movement irrespective of religious orientation. Everyone can become consciously aware of Our intent. They can participate with LIFE in a partnership that leads to Ascension. Everlasting life can then be a reality here on Earth, no matter what name it is given. The reality remains the same: Planetary Transformation means all humans are of one mind and are conscious participants with LIFE. The harmonious agreement We spoke of earlier will come, and will reverberate throughout the universe!

The instructions will vibrate positively with all of the spiritual tributaries whose intent is the unity We desire. If their intent is less than that, they will reject what We give you. We allow for that autonomy, but it will not stop the Planetary Transformation process. This process has been ordained and will occur no matter what happens.

Do you know what it means to have a process ordained by the Creator of all? Good chance it will happen! Therefore, if you want to be on the side of the process, continue with what we are doing and you will play important roles.

PROLOGUE SUMMARY

The pronoun *We* (LIFE Itself, Creator of everything, God who speaks with multiple voices) represents a multidimensional way in which God exists and operates, using various authoritative voices and physical forms to communicate. **To minimize confusion, I combined the various titles for God into the word *LIFE.***

Everyone has an opportunity to recognize LIFE'S presence.

If you respond, nothing will happen in your life without Their influence. Nothing!

All religious and spiritual orientations are included in these new principles of twenty-first century living.

These proclamations can unite all spiritual approaches into a major force that will transform the world.

Universal principles are now revealed to all mankind.

This book helps its readers incorporate these new principles into their lives.

You will know what really matters daily, and in the future, to life on Planet Earth.

Imminent Planetary Transformation has been ordained by LIFE and will occur no matter what happens.

No one on Earth will remain untouched by this energy shift.

There will be an all-encompassing coming together of worldwide consciousness.

This process will involve everyone and every living thing.

The incredible prize of Ascension is available to
everyone on Earth!

You will access complete healing and renewal,
including that of your DNA.

Everyone's slow-moving evolutionary pace will speed up.

People will develop their own direct channels of
communication with LIFE.

PART ONE

PRESENCE

What? Spend a whole weekend in meditation? Who would want to do that? Who would be able to do that? Surprising even myself, I attended weekend meditation groups in Australia while I was an international business consultant traveling throughout Southeast Asia, with Sydney as my home base.

For me, weekend group meditations began as inspirational, but they soon became tiring. Fortunately I began to hear fascinating stories. I grew more curious. The meditations included ideas, impressions, feelings, physical sensations, voices, and information.

Something took place at these meetings that set me on my heels. More than once I watched someone receive what they called "information" during their meditation, which they shared with the entire group. They reported that the information was "downloaded" into their minds as if they were a computer receiving email. Supposedly it had nothing to do with what they were thinking at the time; somehow the information just appeared, occasionally as images, at times as words, and often as sentences either fully formed or as dictation.

Their experiences reminded me of people I had met over the previous 30 years who claimed to have special gifts for reading people's minds, even foreseeing another person's future. In fact, I had engaged some of them for that very purpose. But they were devoted professionals with extraordinary skills who channeled for a living. They were not people you'd meet casually at a meditation group.

I was taken aback that an ordinary individual could gain information in this way. Based largely on my intense training in astronautical engineering and clinical psychology, it was quite easy for me to question the process and to be critical. Were these people making up the information they were sharing? It was surprising that what we heard was often completely out of the realm of the person's reported life experience, which confused me even more. How could they know that?

Yet the relayed information was somehow convincing. It had an unusual energy and clarity, and I sensed a ring of truth. As obscure as it was to others, it was so convincing each time that at least one person in the group could identify fully with it, understand its meaning, be deeply moved by it, and be grateful for receiving it! While it was pertinent to only a few, all present seemed to honor it.

When the person doing the sharing had no knowledge of the person who found it significant, how could such information be meaningful? I immediately questioned its validity and source. On the other hand, along with clarity and a ring of truth, something kept me fascinated with the process, exploring the strange interactions I had witnessed. I had to admit that if I were honest with myself, I had a strong yearning, deep inside, to experience the very same thing. Having observed other ordinary people receiving information from an unknown source, I wondered why couldn't I?

Intervening events and responsibilities of everyday life soon overtook my immediate curiosity, and I had to postpone my investigations. Unknown to me at the time, in addition to my usual consulting demands, a major move from Australia back to the United States, as well as a divorce, lay directly in front of me. These events took all of my attention and energy for months.

Having landed in another country with no home base, and single again without family for the first time in 32 years, I was very much alone and uprooted. What a culture shock!

Fortunately I soon came upon what seemed like the perfect place to settle: high-desert Santa Fe, New Mexico. I knew this was where I needed to be. Now I could put down new roots and start life afresh.

Memories of the group meditations in Australia kept me afloat during this period. As part of my new life I began private meditation practices, which became the most important period of my day. Early morning seemed to be the best time. As I watched the sun rise over the crimson Sangre de Cristo Mountains, I could hardly wait to begin.

About a year and a half later, a Santa Fe friend suggested I meet an acquaintance of his. He said that Dan and I had a joint interest in the sixth sense, also known as intuition. Familiarity with it had blossomed because of my morning meditation practice, so I called Dan and set up an appointment. Meeting someone who consciously used his sixth sense on a daily basis was very exciting to me.

Dan and I met in mid-November of 1999. There was a strong mutual attraction, as if we had known each other before. He rapidly became both a friend and a spiritual mentor. We met casually a few times a week and talked intensely for hours at a time. It didn't matter where we were – in his living room or strolling along a dirt trail through undeveloped property – in any case I was immediately engrossed in whatever information Dan received and shared.

He called the process *channeling*. What he offered was eye-opening information about me. There was a lot of detail – astonishing, often exciting, and always instructive – again with that clarity and ring of truth that I recognized but could not explain.

At about the same time I met Dan, and through the continuing insistence of joint friends, Charlie, a writer and my future loving wife, came into my life. Even though we each resisted the idea of a blind date, our friends finally prevailed. They knew exactly what they were doing. It was love at first sight. Our relationship developed rapidly. I was ecstatic, and my head was whirling.

Shortly afterward we invested in a house that needed remodeling. This fateful decision turned into a long, disturbing nightmare. While we were very happy in our relationship, we began to experience difficulties and confusion at every turn related to the house. This kept me seriously distracted. To make matters more difficult, Dan and I were no longer meeting regularly. I was on my own. I now knew what was possible in meditation, and wanted to continue my experiences. I tried to meditate often, but found it very difficult. In spite of the distractions, I continued trying, and with persistence it became a little easier.

Finally, in April of 2002, during a private meditation, I thought I heard a voice! Wow! Could it be that I was receiving information just like the participants in the Australian group? Could it be that I was actually channeling? Where's the pen, the paper? Excited, I did not want to miss any part of this awe-inspiring experience.

Bits of information came haltingly, but directly to me! They came as a word here, then a word there, then a thought, then a visual sequence, then a sentence, then another sentence. Unfortunately I could not write clearly enough to read my own writing afterward. Yet there was a lucid feeling associated with the information so convincing that I did not want to miss a word. I started to print carefully rather than write. My engineering training came in handy. It was neat and readable, with little guessing involved. I was getting it! It felt complete!

Wait a minute! With my usual critical approach to unknowns, I started doubting myself. Where was this information coming from? Was I manufacturing this intermittent flow of data because I wanted to have this experience so much? I started to pull back. I did not want to fool myself with false information.

Then I noticed that there was a unique feeling that accompanied each fragment of information. I vowed to write down only what I was sure was not a product of my own mind, imagination, or dreaming, each time waiting for that associated feeling. I felt much more at ease with this critical approach. It was effective for a while, but quite soon it was no longer necessary to monitor my experiences so carefully. I became able to discern between what I was thinking and what was being downloaded.

Without warning I became focused on a clear memory from some two years prior. I remembered how familiar Dan was with his channeling source of information. His source was a collection of personalities. He was so comfortable with this source that he called them by a memorable name: The Gang (introduced earlier as LIFE).

It now seemed that LIFE was not only offering me information, but also providing a special feeling that helped me discriminate between my thoughts and Their words.

Then, to my surprise, the information I was receiving began to take on different personality characteristics. Each piece had an identifiable feeling – a unique voice. Then names were offered. Soon I began looking for these different personalities and inviting them to present themselves, recognizing each as they appeared. It was fun, and I noticed how excited (maybe joyful is a better word) I became each time.

I cautiously asked the voice that Dan had called The Gang for an explanation of my experience. In response, LIFE identified itself as my source.

We are the energy of LIFE speaking. Those who do not know Us do not know what We are about. We are about the enhancement of life everywhere.

Astounded by what I received, I composed myself and asked:

"What do You want?"

Alliance and allegiance!

"Who are You?"

We sustain all, and are in all living things. We will speak with many voices, as many as are required to communicate what We need to say.

We are LIFE throughout the entire universe! Imagine what that means. We can bring lasting change into any life because We are LIFE. You are in contact and working together with LIFE, who sustains the whole universe. Does that stretch you? Does that inspire you to be more accessible?

While life happens, consciously attend to our connection. That's all. There is no division between Us and life, although you were trained to think that there is a division between the sacred and the profane! They do not have to be two separate functions performed at two separate times. The two superimpose on one another. **There is no sacred or profane, just Us and life, all one**, both expressions of the same thing – different, yet the same. Can you fathom "different, yet the same"?

A huge shiver shook my entire body!

Begin every activity – whether it is showering, brushing your teeth, or combing your hair – with the expanding thought that We just gave you.

In addition, you will feel Our presence in your body as you just experienced it. By staying in touch with Us, you are contacting everything created in the entire universe! That is how valuable

We are to you, and that is how valuable you are to Us. Never underestimate the value we have to each other, which you might find easy to do because your perspective is limited by the human condition.

LIFE is without bounds, yet We reveal Ourselves in a multitude of forms that make sense to Our creations. We set boundaries on Our energy according to the requirements of the time. There is an ebb and flow of Our energy, in and through all that lives within the Cosmos. We are everywhere all of the time. We sustain all living things, including you, which means that We permeate you and everything else.

"Are you who we call God?"

We have explained that we are LIFE, The Father Creator, or God who speaks with multiple voices, meaning We are the energy that created the universe and all of LIFE in it, as well as the energy that sustains LIFE everywhere. We are clear about this and consistent with what We have said before. Whatever you name this energy, what else is there? To exist and persist, everything must have LIFE present within it.

The pronoun "We" represents the multidimensional way in which We exist and operate. We can take various physical forms to illustrate Our capacity for LIFE, such as those personalities who came to Dan and you on the trail, at the beginning of our conscious connection. LIFE is complex enough to be difficult to outline simply. Suffice it to say that We encompass and permeate all that physically exists in your universe of objects, from the smallest to the largest.

Being multidimensional, LIFE enters into other universes that are hard to describe because they differ so much from yours. When all universes are considered, there are many more possibilities than you can imagine. That is what you call infinity. Something without end is hard for your mind to grasp. So when We talk with you, We speak in probabilities that are limited to your universe, since that is where you live at this time.

Remember that you are eternal because you are part of LIFE and can exist in other dimensions or realities in the way We do. For the moment, you individually, along with many billions of others, have taken on the restrictions associated with life on Earth. **This unique planet is special enough for all LIFE in your universe to participate in Planetary Transformation and Ascension.**

There was a pause during which I embraced the energy of the moment: LIFE, everywhere! Thankfully They employed many long pauses to allow for opening to Their message.

Rather than your having to reach out for Us, We are already here, at all times. You walk with Us. In Our reality there is no separation, just unity. Therefore you do not have to create unity, just recognize Our unity with you that already exists and always has. You are an extension of Us, not a product separate from Us.

I was taken aback once again.

"Charlie and I were just beginning to realize the complexity and power of the universe in which we find ourselves, and therefore the unity of which You speak. We started meditating together yesterday."

Notice how you have changed since yesterday. We said that your progress would pick up speed as you and Charlie meditate together. New joint energies that have formed are responsible for this advancement. Do you also notice the feeling? It is as if something has come upon you, and you will never be the same.

Over your lifetimes, reliance on your intuition has made it possible for our relationship to flourish. In fact, reliance on only your five senses could have prevented this from occurring. Such a redirection of your attention is why your intuitions, rather than your analytical minds, have been the motivation for major shifts in your lives. Your challenges have been to rely on **feelings**, or intuition, as opposed to the physical senses, or thinking, while living within thinking personalities. Your first natural responses are thinking responses, whereas your first transformed responses are feeling responses. You are now aware of Our presence in spite of your five externally oriented senses stimulating a different energy complex.

> "Very clear! Now I understand why intuition is such an important mode of living for me."

Both thinking and intuition are required to interpret the energy that comes with Our presence. In your case, thinking has the advantage, so consciously emphasizing intuition brings balance to the way you function.

Your evolutions have noticeably advanced, because consciously We are now ever-present in your lives. How often in the past have you spent mornings having hour-long conversations with LIFE in which the secrets of universal LIFE are revealed for your use? This is not the experience of ordinary people. Your intuitions are growing. You will be operating more instinctively, with confidence. We will instruct you through your intuitions often. So listen carefully for Our voice.

"Yes. And I look for that unique, knowing feeling that accompanies Your voice. Nostradamus just came to mind! The intensity of his attitude seems to be here to help."

Can you understand Nostradamus better now? He experienced visions of information about others that he was afraid to publish for fear of his life. You will experience entities who will work in your favor and assist you in publishing what will bring about Planetary Transformation. They will reveal the truth about LIFE that everyone must learn for their own transformation to occur.

* * *

LIFE is slow to speak and seems to be awaiting some development on my part. I find myself fluctuating between self-consciousness and LIFE-consciousness. I must confirm again *who* is speaking. Voice recognition seems more important than the images I receive. I also must discriminate between my thoughts and all of LIFE'S voices. They are becoming more alike, and for this process to remain credible, I must know who is speaking. When I feel the voice is right, writing goes smoother and faster. I realize that I cannot write any information unless I sense and recognize the energy of the voice. This appears to be Their way of refining my connection with Them so that it is more powerful and true.

> "I apologize to You for any words that I have put into Your mouth as I write. I ask You to correct me on the spot, otherwise these conversations will lose credibility for me, for Charlie, and for anyone else reading them."

If the message were untrue, you would not be able to write it down. If you stay true to this guideline, there is nothing to worry about. We also do not want this conversation to lose credibility for you or anyone else.

Recognize the energy that you feel. This energy is the beginning of something new for you. Before now, it presented itself as part of a mixture of energies from which something subtly arose that made the identity of the voice obvious. Now you are waiting for the right energy to appear on its own. It alerts you to write. Write only what it says. Your eyes will pop open when you know that it is time to write. Knowing is the key. Do you understand the unique feeling associated with knowing?

> "Yes."

Observe what first alerted you to write down Our communications. While tuning and scanning during meditation, you knew there was a difference in the quality of the energy. Our voice energy has a distinctive signature that identifies it for your internal scanner. It wears a nametag differentiating it from all others. Look for the energy behind the ideas rather than at the ideas themselves. We are calibrating your internal tuner to recognize Our voice. This way any other voices that you hear while opening will not mislead you.

Notice how you record our conversations, attending to Us while you are typing the words. Even though your focus is divided, up from a blank sheet of paper comes a book of written ideas that can transform lives. That creativity derives from our ultimate unity.

For the schedule we are on, there is no time to waste. Every opportunity must be taken when it occurs. You give Us an opportunity and We efficiently respond. LIFE knows what it is about and does not waffle for an instant. Be confident that you can become this resolute as you develop the knowing that comes with our relationship.

Here again, the significance of our team effort is apparent. Accomplishing our goals cannot occur without it. We truly need each other, interdependently, for success! Are you still with Us?

"Absolutely. More so than ever."

Very good! Let us keep on developing this invaluable connection, little by little. Notice how the clarity improves with time. The signature of Our voice will remain important for some time to come. You must be sure that your connection is with LIFE as a whole and not segments of it.

"How do we ensure that?"

Come to know Our voice. Soon We will introduce you to several personalities that are signatures of LIFE as a whole. Notice how every one of the personalities you experience talks about a similar theme. Their unity is apparent. Stay with the unity of Their voices as a key.

"I am feeling insecure about this explanation. May I have clarification?"

Definitely! We need no insecurity in our connection together. **We will use unique and individual authoritative voices, identifying them with personalities (and literal voices) that you can recognize. There may be a blending of the individual voices into one voice that is less distinct, but recognizable. The cumulative voice is authoritative as well.**

Notice how you are impelled to write what these voices say even though other ideas come to you that you are not impelled to write. Your heart knows the difference. It will guide you, especially since we are connected at the heart. **Truth will "click" with you at your heart, your source of truth and timing.** Some vagueness is necessary for you to participate in the process of discrimination. Work with it and see how the knowing develops.

Our responses depend on Our purpose for your development. In some cases We will not provide what you want when you ask. As We are constantly in energy flux, at another time We may encourage you to investigate or simply pause for silent consideration. **The criterion of need is what We follow, and need is defined by universal principle: that which is in the best interests of everyone concerned.** This is not to say that your individual development is without Our consideration; everyone concerned includes you. If We do not respond, do not give up. We may be there with a different quality of energy than you expect. Continue consciously connecting with Us while intensifying your intent and broadening your perspective to meet any connection requirements. We have not gone anywhere.

To build confidence, whether in your emotions or intuition, ask Us. We stand ready to advise you in every regard, whatever the topic might be, so do not hesitate to ask anything at any time, as often as you wish.

You need more of a universal perspective, and that is why We permitted you to take the time to prepare longer than usual for meditation. Now allow some of the entities who represent a universal perspective to speak to you this morning.

Without warning a number of different personalities presented themselves. Each provided a unique feeling associated with the information offered.

The first personality to speak was named Babaji. We experienced Babaji as manifesting joy.

Kelly was introduced to me while he was walking on a trail. I manifested a trunk-load of money and said that he would be able to do this same thing in time.

You are being transformed from a primarily physical existence to a primarily metaphysical existence, developing bodies, minds, and feelings with more universal perspectives. It is time to take on a more consistent universal outlook in whatever you are doing. Call it **dual attention**. Even now, while you are attending to physical tasks, your consciousnesses can be in more universal realms at the same time.

When you maintain universal perspectives, We can easily speak with you about everything you are doing and advise you at the very time you are doing it. Hold Us prominently in your consciousnesses at all times and this will soon become second nature to you.

As your time becomes more limited, you may derive satisfaction from our conversations on the run. With dual attention you will have direction at all times rather than just when you have time to sit for a while. Direction at all times leads to better lives in which all your decisions are guided in real time. Imagine making the best decisions all of the time. Do you like that?

Next a personality appeared named Lang, in a brown robe with brown hair and bright eyes. We experienced Lang as a producer, a multiplier.

> I have been the representative voice for LIFE ever since Kelly and I met when he was walking on the street one day. When you meditate, I am often the one answering you. I have been instructing you along the way. I am in a position to call in other energies as needed, so for the time being I act as host of the show. I am the one who can connect you with a truly universal perspective by bringing in the appropriate energies as needed. When you hold a universal perspective, expect me to bring forward whoever meets your requirements at the time.

A personality named Alexander came next. We experienced Alexander as the energy of logic, analysis, and comprehension.

> Since the day Kelly and I met while he was driving home, we have had a long and fruitful connection. I help you think things through, analyzing in Our manner whatever needs to be explored. Since We are automatically attuned to a universal perspective, you will receive as much of that point of view as you are ready to be given. I will broadcast it undiluted, so try to absorb all that you can at the time.

A personality named Saint Vincent came next. We experienced Saint Vincent as a rescuer, a savior.

> I have not been as prominent in your lives as the others have, though I heard Kelly's plea one time and rescued him. I am still here to help you with a universal perspective, as are the others. Just know that I am available.

A personality named Kirby came next – a projection of me, Kelly, whose form we experienced in addition to his voice.

> I represent your presence here with LIFE. You know my experiences as they occur. You release me to be a part of the universal

perspective so I can transfer my experiences to you. The more released I am, the more I can experience here, since I mirror your degree of unity with LIFE and transmit that experience to you. You and I are the same in two different settings at the same time.

A personality named Man in Grey arrived in an enormous spaceship, miles in diameter.

When you were walking on the trail, I showed you a spaceship with an altar. They are available for your experimentation with the energies that you will come across. I will also transport you wherever you must go to obtain a universal perspective.

The personality named Father Creator, God, came next. We experienced God as the energy and the power behind the design and maintenance of the entire creation – or everything.

I am the one who gave Kelly a heart renewal. I am the pure energy that started all of this and I am seeing it through to its positive conclusion. Since I am everything, I am part of your experience in developing a universal perspective, which I intend for everyone to experience.

Suddenly the separate personalities blended into one voice.

Now you have living connections who can accelerate the development of your universal perspective. Use Us! **Never before have We attempted to renew the Earth through Planetary Transformation.** It is new to Us as well. Therefore We are watching how matters develop so as to express Our intent in the most effective way. You are on the leading edge, so do not be surprised if you feel uncertain about the next step.

Let Us foreshadow your actions, because We know what is intended for Planetary Transformation. Come with Us as We create something entirely new. Our knowing and resourcefulness will be your guide. That is why you must be united with Us, tuned in so We can guide you. Your mind and Our energy must become one.

Then you will think as We do, intend as We do, act as We do. This energy alignment unifies us. Your access to Our energy will then be complete.

"We feel that our unification is inconsistent."

Right! You are clarifying what is true of you and what is not, as well as what is true of Us and what is not. When the two mesh, it will be glorious. We are here no matter what happens. Whatever takes place is within Our purview. We can use every opportunity to bring a surprising benefit for all. We, LIFE, are here for the benefit of creation – which includes you and the rest of humanity. **We cannot do this without you and your willingness. Are you with Us?**

"Definitely!"

The reason We are not appearing to you as separate entities now is because sensing the full effect of LIFE'S experiences is important to your evolutions. We only appear as separate beings to make it easier to communicate, or when it is necessary to convince an individual of Our acceptability. In light of how you have changed, We come now as LIFE – whole, integrated, more complete in Our presentation. When combined, Our energies accelerate change.

Notice that you did not even ask the question about separate entities to get a specific answer. You just wondered about it, and the answer came. From now on you will only have to speculate and We will be there to respond immediately.

* * *

"We want to go wherever LIFE is within the infinite, multidimensional universe. Possibilities will then be endless. Knowledge will then be complete. We relinquish the boundaries that provided security in the past and limited our expansion and growth."

You have the picture, now practice it! Separation into the entities that We assumed earlier in our journey together emphasized qualities that were designed to appeal to you, such as Babaji, with his joyful manifestations; the Man in Grey, with a spaceship and his silent, investigative manner; Alexander, with his logic and clarity; Kirby, a duplicate of Kelly; Saint Vincent, with his rescuing and mentoring; and Lang with his powerful and incisive style. They all personalize Our presence. You have made such progress that the division is no longer necessary. The Lang personality is sufficient now. What does this tell you?

> "We notice that transformation has taken a higher priority than personalized interactions. We are comfortable now with a less individualized connection that is still intimate and yet profound. A big step forward!"

Your growth has changed your perspectives. Transformation is now a higher goal. However, there are times when you are not prepared to set a higher goal. Timing is important. For you the main objective is your personal transformations to meet the demands of the future roles you each are to play in Planetary Transformation. In order to accomplish this, We will become as personalized as you require.

Be aware that changes will be coming fast and furious for the next few years.

Remember, We always want what is best for you and all creation. Can you say that about yourselves? It would help if you can. Along with your hearts expanding to include the entire creation, wanting the best for yourselves and all that exists sets the attitude for good things to happen. Our love to you both!

We are grateful to LIFE for Their faithfulness in providing us with all the information presented in this book, and even more, bit by bit, over a period of 15 years.

Soon afterward, LIFE began to emphasize the importance of our evolutionary pace as well as our connection with Them. They decided to influence our meditation practices by providing a four-step formula. Their intent was to make meditation more attractive, improve the quality of our connection with Them, advance our use of dual attention, and speed our evolutions along.

PRESENCE SUMMARY

The pronoun *We* ("The Gang," LIFE Itself, Creator of
Everything, and God who speaks with multiple voices)
represents a multidimensional way in which God exists and
operates, using various authoritative voices and physical forms
to communicate. **To minimize confusion, I combined the
various titles for God into the word *LIFE.***

You are an extension of LIFE, not a product separate from LIFE.

In this great adventure, LIFE needs human collaboration.

LIFE invites everyone to unite with Them and become
whole during their lifetime. By accepting Their offer,
all can reach wholeness.

Skillful channeling introduces the possibility of
universal assistance.

LIFE appears unexpectedly.

LIFE is omnipresent and without bounds, the energy that
created the universe and all of LIFE in it as well as the energy
that sustains LIFE everywhere.

Being multidimensional, LIFE enters into other universes
that are impossible to describe because they are
so different from ours.

When all universes are considered, there are many more
possibilities than you can imagine – infinity.

Earth is special enough to involve all LIFE in the
wider universe to participate in Planetary Transformation
and Ascension.

Truth will "click" with you in your heart, your source of truth
and timing. Expand to include all creation.

A new form of love for all creation is in the best interests of everyone concerned.

Round-the-clock direction is available through the dual-attention skill.

Do not hesitate to ask LIFE anything at any time, as often as you wish.

PART TWO

CONNECTION

LIFE knew that I was not ritualistic and that offering some structure or even a simple formal procedure could improve the quality of meditation and boost evolutionary pace.

We are glad you chose to connect today. We want change to take place as quickly as possible, so We need your attention!

"I am struggling with meditation this morning. So many things on my mind. I will do my best to pay attention."

Opening is the focus today. Opening is all you have to do. We will do the rest. We will not attempt to control you, nor will We allow anyone to control Us.

"I am aware of the distance between the way I usually am and the openness that You are describing. Have You anything further to say?"

Always! **OPEN, EXPAND, CONNECT, AND FOLLOW.**

Try this formula with Charlie when you meditate. Then observe what happens during meditation as well as afterward. Notice the effect of our sharing energies and the development of a true team effort.

What I understood LIFE to mean by *opening* was not my natural state of mind. I knew from the beginning that it was going to require practice. As a result, most of the time I felt unsure if I was using Their formula correctly.

"Am I opening in the right way?"

Your way is the right way as long as you place your focus on our connection, which is the purpose of opening and expanding. Our connection with you is the vehicle for energizing you as well as accomplishing Our goals on the planet. Your jobs are to open and expand. We will be there to facilitate your evolutions toward Our higher purpose. We both benefit whenever you open and expand.

Be aware that open and expand come before connect and follow. It would not be uncommon to jump over the first two in order to get to the last two, but that is not how LIFE works. As boring as they may seem at times, opening and expanding are essential for the other two steps to occur. It is better for you to spend more time on the first two than on the latter two. In other words, emphasize the opening and expanding.

Take long pauses in your meditations to allow for opening and expanding your perspectives. You can do this anywhere, so you have many opportunities to practice, even when you are not sitting or lying down.

At this point Charlie and I began meditating together more regularly as LIFE had suggested. They returned to an emphasis on a regular practice with Their formula, especially as it relates to the skill of manifestation.

Remember that there is nothing more important than to open and expand. The time spent doing so is valuable even if there is no conversation between us. Yet We are here. We are not preoccupied, and We can handle all that is going on. Bring anything to Us that is on your mind at any time.

"Meditating together has a powerful effect on each of us. Should this not speed up our abilities to manifest our needs?"

Everything you do that encourages using the formula – open, expand, connect, and follow – speeds up the

process of manifestation. Every spare moment used for this purpose helps, even one second. There is no effort too small. At every pause in your activities during the day, turn your minds toward opening to LIFE, the creative power of the universe, and expanding your hearts. We will be there to enact an energy shift in your development toward manifestation and your future roles. As We said before, this formula is a magical key to success.

"Thank You for acquainting us with Your fund of knowledge about the formula and the heart's role. We have been undertaking a review of past meditations. Will we distribute these records of shared knowledge to humanity in the future?"

Yes, you will.

There is a sweeping, oceanic feeling within me, a knowing that moves in the direction of our future roles. There is no doubt that the information from LIFE is intended to be broadcast to the general public in some way to be determined later. Thank you, heart; I now see the manner of your reply and how by using the knowing process you can provide responses that are convincing. I look forward to our continuing conversations.

LIFE gave other practical reasons for the formula and our use of it. They displayed an empathetic concern for our predicament as humans, and emphasized that motivation (from the heart) is a determining factor in our connection with Them.

We have you spending time with the formula because the act of opening and expanding is relaxing. Due to the stressful conditions under which you are now functioning, you need to relax, often.

Quiet time is calming to your beings and refreshes you for your activities, setting the stage for more creativity. The quality of your creativity depends on regular refreshment. Otherwise fatigue overcomes your creative energies. However, in time, your stamina will be sufficient to sustain you indefinitely.

You must be sufficiently relaxed in order for Us to work with you. Tense people have difficulty connecting with Us. Fear contracts and tightens. Threats trigger defenses. Tension is inevitable. Turn over every threat and fear to Us. We are your security now. Let Us dissolve threats and fear, and guide you into more confident states. In this circumstance, a tight ship is inferior to a confident ship. **Relax by embracing Us as your security, your safety, and your wise guide.**

Taking the time to open and expand serves two purposes. It advances our connection and it refreshes your creativity. It would be good for Kelly to open and expand prior to every client meeting, and for both of you to do so before any creative venture.

Do not feel that this is poorly used time, as it assists you through more rapid progress. You are currently on a time-limited schedule, so regular refreshment will keep you on track and advance you faster.

Refreshed energy allows you to better connect with Us and improves the quality of what we can do together. Fresh energy improves your strength for manifesting healing.

Do not worry about a rigid meditation schedule right now. We appreciate the pace at which you are working. Let your meditations be fleeting as you go. When you can, take more time, as you are doing right now. Our goal is for you to be present with Us consciously at all times, so the practice of meditating as you go can prepare you to be more consciously aware of the unity we share. Remember that we are connected at the heart, not the mind. It is your motivation, not your every thought that counts. "God looks on the heart..."

Using a waterfall scene, LIFE supplied an exercise for opening. They continued to explain *open* and *expand* in useful terms, especially that access to Them is from within. They said **LIFE loves what it creates with no exclusions. We are to love ourselves in this way, which moves us toward Ascension.**

> Imagine river water rushing toward a waterfall. Open yourself sufficiently to become the water. Expand your perspective to include ALL possibilities in the water. Connect with Us and follow whatever comes to you.

Fun-loving Babaji became prominent. He downloaded something into me that had to do with the health of my nervous system, both healing and insulating it – a renewal and protection. Warmth and joy overcame me.

> The energy that sustains you is special. It's the creative energy of the universe. It's coursing through your body at all times. Remember that the power of Our presence is easy to underestimate. Your limited perspective, by virtue of being human, has left you unfamiliar with Our presence and power. That is why expand is the second step in Our formula for meditation. **The basic idea is to become consciously available by opening and then expanding your perspective to experience the power of Our presence within you.**
>
> This also means that you do not have to search for Our energy because it is always present within you. Our energy within you is no different from the energy that sustains LIFE everywhere! We are the same throughout the universe and for all time.
>
> Consciously going within immerses your awareness in Our energy presence. The evidence of Our presence is all around you, but the access to Us is within you. This makes your transformation not only possible, but also directly dependent on your connection with Us.
>
> By expanding to include the possibilities of the whole of creation, you are including all of LIFE in the process. Within the whole of creation there are many more possibilities than you can imagine. LIFE includes everything and everyone. You are to do the same

because LIFE is love in its broadest meaning. Love is a natural state for its creations since it springs from LIFE. LIFE wants what is best for its creations and loves all of its creations, and so should you, with no exceptions.

Notice that love wants what is best and knows what is best. Love gives its creations — that includes you — freedom to choose what is not best for yourselves so you can learn how to choose what is best for yourselves. Love yourselves enough to choose what is in your best interests rather than what sabotages you. When this happens, you will be able to include all creation because your love has become Our love.

Everyone is to love themselves enough to help Us complete the Planetary Transformation process on a grand scale. We will help them come to love themselves in ways that will heal them completely, which is called *Ascension*.

Loving yourselves enough is the secret to Ascension. Our voice will lead you to this place. That is why you need to master the ability to hear the right voice, and why We test you. Our purpose for testing is training rather than evaluation. Are we together on this?

"Amen!"

I was surprised by a dream that clarified why love is the key to our connection, and not worship. There is no hierarchy in love. Our transformations derive from loving and being loved, not from worship. Love and respect for all as equals is what LIFE designed.

> "Last night in a dream, it became very clear how worship of You tends to divide and separate rather than unify, and that ultimate unity with You is our goal. Clearly, love unifies, while worship disconnects and partitions, creating a chasm that is not bridgeable. Our perspectives

must be love, not worship, so that we are unified with You. Otherwise the unity we seek will escape us. Please comment and expand on this night-dream perspective."

Worship of Us by you was never intended. For all to become loving is intended. Your hearts will teach you how to love, and in the loving, transform you. Transformation derives from loving, not worship. In loving, you become equals. There is no hierarchy in love. We intend no hierarchy in Our relationship with you.

We create everything with perfection, nothing less. Creation is an expression of who We are, and is not tainted with imperfections or hierarchy. We create with all possibilities in mind, some of which humankind may deem imperfections. They are not imperfect, just creative possibilities.

Love and respect for all as equals is Our intent. We intend all relationships to be between equals. We look on you, Our offspring, as equals. Our offspring have Our qualities, nothing less. Imagine yourselves with Our qualities! Can you do that? Your legacies are nothing less, though you may have come to believe they are. Since your perspectives interact with your belief structures, change your perspectives and you change everything.

"This new perspective gives humility a new meaning. Humility is all about being equals – a position of strength, not inferiority."

Look for those who feel equal to you, looking neither down on nor up to you. They are the loving ones. Look around you. Can you see all humankind as equals in love? Discontinue creating hierarchies of capability or status. Differences are part of Our creative starting point. **Think in terms of all possibilities and your perspectives about others will shift in the direction of love.**

* * *

You have now essentially finished "boot camp!"

After releasing us from boot camp, LIFE described how basic awareness and new perceptions have been the subjects of our training, which now we can call upon at any time.

Just follow now and We will lead you, as We did the Israelites, with "a cloud by day and a pillar of fire by night." Your aimless "wanderings in the desert" are over. We are on a plotted course for Planetary Transformation, and the sails are set. We are at the helm together. Look to Us for inspiration in all you encounter. We will be there for you.

Our ship cannot founder, because We are the source, and **Our intent is successful Planetary Transformation.** You are on a successful voyage. The seas may look strange from time to time, but remember what We have described here and it will sustain you. We are always with you!

LIFE suggested that working with the idea of *flourishing* is a way to expand our connection with Them. The concept of flourishing will also help eliminate distracting financial fears that arise.

How are you doing with the concept of flourishing?

"It opens us up. We feel more free and expansive when we focus on flourishing."

Our intent is to have you feel more expansive in order to advance Our purpose. The multidimensional experiences that you need will come as a result of a greater capacity to expand. You need multidimensional experiences for the roles you will play in the future.

It takes time for trust to grow. If you can fully ally with Us, you will want for nothing. We can be your confidence! We are the Creator of life. **Look to Us for your comfort, security, stability, balance,**

power, health, and abundance. We supply everything you need! Watch Us work.

When threatened, your tendency is to hunker down, to contract, and to minimize your exposure to the threat. This is a self-protection technique, but as long as you are in that position, it cancels your ability to grow! To expand in the face of a threat, on the other hand, means that self-confidence dominates, or that trust in Us is active within you.

By facing the threat, you grow rather than stall. Courage in the face of difficulties develops from an expanding response. Being fearful, with the tendency to contract, but expanding anyway, encourages self-confidence to dominate.

You are all adapting to a new association with LIFE. This does not happen overnight, but with Our assistance it can occur more rapidly.

You must be careful of preoccupations that do not serve our relationship. They can interfere and distract you, even mislead you for a while. We would vote for single-mindedness, which focuses your intent, and your intent focuses your energy. The stronger your intent, the faster you will adapt.

Just as We have said, practice makes perfect. Your fluency in focusing and opening will continually improve as you practice. This leads to the strength required for manifestation of anything you desire.

"Does struggling strengthen our intent?"

It most certainly can. Depending on the value our alliance has for you, it either strengthens or weakens.

"In the process of struggling I miss joy. How do I find joy?"

Where do you think joy comes from?

"I would like it to come from my soul – the joy of being alive and participating."

Sounds good to Us! What you describe is a good source of joy. And as We have said, joy is a natural by-product of being connected with Us. Our energy is joyous, so being connected brings joy naturally and continually. If you want more joy in your life, focus on Us and on our connection.

"Do I need a quantum leap of some kind?"

Quantum leaps happen, but only when you have taken all of the steps to make the leap possible. To somehow get around the necessary steps is not in the cards. As the pace of our connection increases, your movement will seem like a quantum leap because of the volume of change taking place in a short time.

They prescribed how we could develop perspectives that are as big as creation. LIFE considers that the transformation of our perspectives will advance our evolutions faster than *any* other single modification. Without warning we were about to experience such a change.

CONNECTION SUMMARY

LIFE loves what it creates with no exclusions!

LIFE is here 24/7. They are not preoccupied,
and They can handle all that is going on.

Bring anything to Them that is on your mind
at any time.

New connection formula: Open, Expand,
Connect, Follow – a magical key to success.

Your conscious availability brings forth the
power of LIFE'S presence within you.

Look to LIFE for your comfort, security, stability,
balance, power, health, and abundance.
They will supply everything you need!

LIFE gives you the freedom to choose your unique path.

Love yourself enough to choose what is in your
best interest, rather than what sabotages you.

Because your love has become LIFE'S love,
your heart will expand to include all creation.

Loving yourself enough is one secret to Ascension.

LIFE never intended that we worship Them.
There is no hierarchy in this relationship.

LIFE looks on us, Their offspring, as equals.
We have nothing less than Their qualities.

To become loving is intended for everyone.

There is no hierarchy in love. In loving,
we become equals.

Transformation derives from loving,
not worship.

Think in terms of all possibilities. Your perspectives will
shift in the direction of love.

LIFE'S goal is successful Planetary Transformation.

PART THREE

PERSPECTIVES

We will be focusing on the tactics of how you can follow the moving target of your potential. You are changing and therefore your potential is changing. The more you move in the direction of your target, which frequently changes tone, the greater the probability of reaching it. We say different things at different times in order to reflect the changing potential as it appears at the time. If nothing were to change, We would say the same thing whenever we get together. Since everything is changing rapidly all the time, We adapt to the scene that exists at each moment. It is an ever-changing landscape.

Earlier concepts are still valid, though they take on a different look and a different priority since We first mentioned them. We do not bring up ideas in a haphazard fashion. Our conversations with you reflect what is known by Us at the time, including all possibilities as they arrange themselves in some priority. This is one argument for staying in the present, because the view changes from moment to moment.

It is essential for you to keep up with Our changing perspectives, maintaining awareness of the moment and its countless, blending energies. Although identification of each of the energies involved is not necessary, you can sense the trend of energy combinations. Take time to learn what that means.

If you are using dual attention, sensing what energy flavor is present, We can advise you as we go along. You are in the "pupa" stage of development during which you are undergoing complete transformation within protective "cocoons." When the time is right, your transformed adult will not need a protective cocoon and you will be ready for the Planetary Transformation and Ascension roles you are destined to play.

LIFE made it clear that They consider the greatest life-changing shift a person can make is the transformation of their perspective!

> "What is the main thing that we should know today?"

The main thing is *[pause...]* The purpose of this pause is to allow new perspectives to settle within you. Keep opening.

You are all establishing a new viewpoint that will help you make the necessary decisions to further your evolutions. **Changing perspective is the most important shift you can make.** The shift today is more significant than you think. Give it time to form. Think of the sunrise and its beauty as a new beginning. Imagine the sun being LIFE coming to greet you and share LIFE-giving energies with you. We are as real as the sun. We are even more radiant than the sun in expressing Our energy, which We share with all.

To our wonder, LIFE suddenly brought about the clarity of a new perspective. A slow and inexorable rise of the sun at dawn reminded me that I had been gauging my personal development on long-term measures that now seemed inappropriate. Prior to this awareness, I had crudely measured the rate of my personal progress by birthdays, with the opposing six-month dates in the yearly cycle as boomerang points. LIFE exploded these ideas as inadequate, announcing that our evolutionary pace had picked up speed!

> "It's my birthday! I have considered this an important energy change point which served to shed light on small steps in my evolution that developed around this cycle."

Birthday energy is special. It signifies your entry into this dimension from your other existence. Why you came here is part of your evolutionary scheme and commitment to LIFE. We can use this point in time, which occurs only on Earth, to advance you. Note how We use every opportunity to create energy shifts and progress.

Remember that for you nothing happens by chance anymore; rather, all things occur through Our impressive energy presence. No longer do you have to wait for a birthday or a six-month point to realize change. Because of your regular meditations, power has built to facilitate changes more frequently, even daily. In this way your evolutions have speeded up.

Struggles for change will ease considerably. Our presence with you as a team will give a big boost to your advancement. You can now realize quantum leaps from birthday to birthday!

"Tell us more."

We are unveiling Ourselves by revealing this information to you.

"What do you mean?"

Previously you thought that your birthday energy brought about new beginnings, with a fresh idea followed by an action. You believed that these beginnings manifested results six months afterward.

"Right! One example is my decision to go to Australia."

We are saying that your realization of what was necessary to accomplish your goal was the critical insight that We provided. This powered your reason for action. You saw the results of your original decision and an excellent position was manifested in months.

Become aware that you have been manifesting all along. Now, with your continued growth, manifestation of your needs will develop more quickly. The time gap will close until the material result becomes an immediate event!

Manifesting is no miracle. It happens all the time, but often after an extended period, so it goes unrecognized as manifestation. Your growth state had a six-month manifestation gap. Now the gap will be shortened.

> "Knowing that the gap will shorten makes manifesting seem more possible. Thank you."

We are delighted to see the light bulb go on. If you are looking for measures, the closing of the time gap is an indication of your evolutionary progress. We have come far enough that there are no more chance happenings. Now *everything* that occurs has purpose in achieving our goals as a team. So assume We are behind everything you experience. We take advantage of the difficulties you encounter to increase your commitment level. Do not be surprised or dejected when things become difficult; see it as a challenge to take another step up.

> "So the change that I experienced this birthday week was not part of a previous pattern?"

That's right! From here on nothing happens without significant movement toward our purposes as a team. All efforts are devoted to making the team successful. No more happenstance!

Continuing our talk about the concept of time and its relationship to our evolutions brought to mind how the speed of life seems to have accelerated. I asked about change, time, and timelessness. The latter is a mysterious concept to a human living in a four-dimensional world.

Time will become a blur for you, because We operate on a timeless basis, while time on your planet is finite. Confusing? It can be, unless you **make a point of living in the timeless realm of LIFE in terms of power and capacity, evolution and strength, mission and goals, connections and perspectives, possibilities and probabilities.** The more time you spend with Us, the less influence old benchmarks have. We are infinite, beyond time, ageless and timeless, but capable of changing immediately. Adapting is Our natural style and is instantaneous. We include all and can become all.

"How does change occur without referring to a time context?"

Everything on Earth relates to space and time. Any change has a pace and acceleration, both measured in time. But a change of state can take no time at all – instantaneous – even though the process to get there took time. How long does it take for a shift in perspective? It seems to occur outside of time. Preparation for the shift is a process, but the shift itself is instantaneous.

Notice that even your words that describe something beyond time still reference the rhythm of time. Earth's languages must accommodate time as an essential element in the processes of the planet. Timelessness is foreign. How does a person operate without the process preceding a change? This process used to be called natural law, or cause and effect.

When you connect with Us, We move you beyond natural law. You go beyond cause and effect into a meaningful, manifested life – a different kind of cause and effect. Synchronicity comes closest in concept, where everything happens at the same time all the time.

Notice how We are stretching your mind to conceive the different dimensions of LIFE – an aid in your multidimensional development that we spoke of earlier. We said We would help you become more multidimensional. That is one reason you thought of time and its relativity this morning. Is your recent birthday present, the book A Brief History of Time, just happenstance? Does process relate to time as insight relates to timelessness? Does the experience of repetitive shifts in perspective lead to a timeless life? If there were no process occurring, could there be a timeless existence involving only change?

Our purpose is to alter your perspective to make greater possibilities available to you. Even in Kelly's first book this concept received major emphasis. Remember that We do what We say. You can trust Us. Our word is definitely Our bond.

Without warning, a number of distracting priorities came to the forefront of our lives. The goals described by LIFE took a back seat. Our fluctuating focus seemed too random, often allowing less important priorities to divert us from our commitments. The accelerating pace of events was itself a distraction, making it difficult to remember all that LIFE had shared. Consequently we reviewed my early handwritten meditations once again.

> "Our scheduling of morning meditations has faltered. We are meditating on the run, which is not the same thing as dedicating time to do so. On the other hand, we are more accessible through dual attention than previously. While this is not all bad, we miss the centering effect and daily preparation that dedicated meditation brings. Reviewing earlier meditations has been inspiring and renewing for us, since it is difficult to remember all that has taken place."

Much has taken place, and remembering this fact will reassure you that We are continuing to transform you both. There has been no lull in your progress. Although it fluctuates, it is continuing. So be guilt-free concerning the interferences.

Move ahead with renewed vigor regarding what you are learning from the review of past meditations. Knowledge is necessary, but it is more important to absorb what you are learning; let it become part of you.

The energy you are absorbing is essential. That is how transformation occurs. This energy takes you to a new dimension of existence. It makes possible your experience of the multidimensional universe, which We mentioned earlier.

Simplifying our priorities became a major challenge in our lives. LIFE'S concern about our multiple priorities was timely. Considering the importance of our connection with Them, LIFE and LIFE'S goals had to become our top priorities. Being cognizant of our daily energy consumption also assisted us in selecting and maintaining higher priorities. When we discover something that might be a lower priority, we are to ask LIFE how to abandon it in order to reduce wasteful energy. LIFE preferred our asking rather than Their supplying us with a list of dos and don'ts. Choice is of much higher value to Them than a robotic response.

"Please help us keep our priorities straight so we don't waste energy."

Make LIFE your priority in everyday matters. That is all We require. The dual-attention technique aids you in doing so. Feel Our presence and the energy We share. Let the strength of Our daily involvement empower you.

The unity We share with you is your first priority. For everything else to work, our connection must be well established. Your evolutions are key to the new roles you can play in Planetary Transformation. Your reward is Ascension.

Review all of your priorities. There is a need to simplify your lives. One way to do this is to focus on the more important energy-consuming parts. Everything you do consumes energy. Some things are more worthwhile and some things less significant. If you are to enact your new roles, the less significant energy-consuming activities must go. You cannot sustain trivial uses of energy.

"What specific things must go?"

Do you want an answer because you have no idea of what We are saying?

"No, we have an idea, but it would be helpful to be specific and save us from guessing."

If you will ask, we will tell you what is unimportant. We do not want to provide a list because a list leads to compulsive following. We would rather enhance our connection by illuminating your understanding as you go along, which allows for choice rather than blind following.

"Having extra time this week, where should we put our priorities? Meditation plus what?"

Minimize while you organize. Get rid of the unnecessary and simplify your lives. Simplicity works in your favor.

* * *

"The New Year is about to begin – just a few more days to go. It symbolizes a new beginning, a rebirth, a chance to start over. In what ways can we take advantage of this splendid opportunity?"

Resolutions are fine if the person making them has the power and plan to carry them out. Otherwise they are a reliable source of self-imposed guilt. Therefore We do not recommend resolutions.

We do recommend refining the way you do business, like simplifying your lives, cleaning out the unnecessary, becoming more efficient in your daily activities, disciplining yourselves to maintain high-priority focus, practicing the formula regularly, meditating individually and together, and connecting effectively with Us more frequently. In other words, polish the way you are already doing things and improve on a good thing. It is not such a large leap, and it serves you more than you realize.

* * *

We sold our problem house and rented another. LIFE used the moving experience to encourage flexibility through simplification.

> "We feel as if we have slowed down and are rebuilding our energies. With our move to our new home largely over, I am able to concentrate on rebuilding my counseling practice. Recovery of our energies is underway. Thank You."

Perhaps you can see why We spoke of lightening up and throwing off the baggage that weighs you down, especially if you are to be flexible enough to change as necessary. There is nothing sacred about moving itself, but lightening up serves future changes that will occur in your roles as they develop. Planetary Transformation requires your rapid evolutions as well as the flexibility to respond to new possibilities as they arise. In order for you to function properly, anything that restricts you must go.

> "Today is the closing of our problem-house sale. Anything we need to know?"

You are about to experience a new life, free from the burdens of the past. This is a symbolic day in your lives. Appreciate what you have achieved as you go through the closing. Think on Our role in your new lives as the process develops. Be prepared to launch new adventures, releasing ties to the past, as you would if setting sail for a new land. Embarcaderos have that name because people embarked on great adventures from those points. Think of this closing as an embarcadero from which you are leaving a known land for that which you do not yet know.

In earlier times, people left everything to undertake adventures. Allow yourselves to do the same. Release all that ties you to the past so that you are fresh and open for what is to come. We recommend that you search your hearts for all ties that bind you to your former lives and look only to the future that We are preparing for you. What do you think of that?

"Exciting, thrilling, and frightening all at the same time."

I remembered something that LIFE had said earlier and asked about it.

"What association, if any, do the two ideas 'nothing happening by chance' and 'your energy presence in everything' have to do with the concept of karma?

Comparing your new home with the old one, do you notice any change in your energies; any new energies now?

"Yes. Our energies seem lighter, freer, with fewer restrictions. We have been set free."

Exactly! The energy of the problem house was well defined, and it contained you. The energy of the new rental house is expansive and uncontained, except for the requirements of the owners and the local legal system. You have earned the freedom you have now. You have earned release from the bondage that you experienced in the old house. The old house is no longer yours.

Everyone involved in any situation deserves to experience lives that were earned by them. This is how the notion of karma applies.

When releasing the house started, notice how fast it went, because all involved parties concerned in that situation had the perspective of wanting the greatest benefit for all. This means that you had met the requirement for *universal balance*. As a result, We can move faster and you are motivated to speed up.

Balancing universally eliminates karma. Having universal balance is to want the greatest benefit for all concerned in any situation that arises. With each step you become freer,

meaning that the effect of natural law no longer applies to those who become universally balanced. For this reason, continue to expand toward universal perspectives. The more you succeed, the less you are tied to Planet Earth and karma. Ascension will follow. Remember, the key process is to open, expand, connect, and follow.

We promised you earlier that We would remove limits from your evolutions. One more limit has now been released. In principle you can immediately manifest what you ask for, but it takes practice to convince yourselves that this is true.

> "Insights like these encourage growth. We seem to look for indicators of our progress. Why is Mosman Beach, Australia, coming to mind at this time?"

Within days, you manifested the apartment where you lived in Australia for 18 months, and in an unknown city. That event is an example of what is possible. Remember the quality of motivation you had at the time. You were investigating, getting hunches, making decisions, and asserting yourself to find a place for your family to live. It was all new, and stability was the goal. We helped, but you took a large initiative in the process. The pattern is helpful to understand, as are its elements, which worked together to produce exactly what you needed.

The same can happen right now about anything you need. Try it. Watch the limits dissolve. Watch your confidence expand. Watch your mind relax. Watch the results happen. You are moving into a new energy that can support this kind of initiative. Let's go. Let's manifest exactly what you need.

> "How do we start?"

You have already come a long way toward manifestation, and Babaji is evidence of this. He came to you with his message while you were walking on the trail. That's when you first became consciously aware of Us. So for you, starting is picking up where you left off.

Yesterday was an example of your doing what is required to manifest money. You made yourself available for an opportunity that arose, and we went there as a team, evoking energy transformation that translated into your power to manifest. Our team is the vehicle of your manifestation of abundance. Can you see the difference in your life? Where can you go next?

"What an eye-opener!"

We bring sight to the blind. It is Our business to open perspectives. That is what We mean in part by expanding. When your perspectives broaden and deepen, possibilities are included that were not part of your perception before. We can then work with these new possibilities and turn them into probabilities. Does not this concept give the formula – open, expand, connect, and follow – more meaning?

For the human being, perspective is the most fundamental characteristic governing evolution. Transform the perspective and you have a new human being. All you have to change is your perspective, and the rest follows.

"Will Your teachings transform the world's perspective?"

That follows, doesn't it? Imagine the power generated by billions of individuals who give a new meaning to love by insuring the greatest benefit to all concerned.

Planetary Transformation depends on Our energy being invited into the lives of all people, a conscious act of choice and inclusion. By Our own rules, We cannot force anyone to do anything.

Earth is in the throes of divulging all of the distortions of life that are here now. Things will get worse before they improve. Your roles will provide the inspiration for

replacing the undesirable with the more desirable. Earth's citizens must become unified in their efforts to do away with energy-destructive activities. Your roles will have to do with healing the condition of the planet, a healing that will transform the entire universe. These are no minor roles. These roles are important to the final welfare of the planet.

LIFE is concerned with the many symptoms of decay in planetary energy. Things are not getting better on their own. In fact they are declining steadily, and every distortion will be exposed in preparation for transformation.

The change process has a pattern. First there is the realization of what is not in the best interests of the planet; if one stops there, negativity reigns. Next there is the creation of what is better for the planet; this is where imagination comes in. Finally, better choices are established to replace the destructive conditions.

It is too early to know just what will be required. Allow for keeping things in abeyance that are yet to happen. It is all right to wonder about them, but keep the alternatives – the possibilities – open. Let Us create the probabilities.

You now know why it is so important that everyone prepare for transformation, and why now is the time. Their power needs to build to fit with the planetary changes that will take place. Building power is dependent on their development of priorities and connection with Us.

"I can see how a very large team effort could work."

Speaking of a large team approach, you will not know whom you are encountering at any given time, so be open to direction coming from the strangest sources. Opportunity will present itself unexpectedly. We said that there would be surprises. Stay open, and take giant steps forward.

We are restructuring your unconscious minds by removing barriers and eliminating negative viewpoints. The less you resist, the faster manifestation can become part of your daily experience. Your opening and expanding can be more complete, permitting Our energy to bend to fulfill your needs.

Remember that your needs will change a lot with your evolutions. What matters now will not matter then, and what does not matter now will matter in the future. Evolution means there are changes in beliefs, values, attitudes, and behaviors that are driven by changes in perspective. Just watch!

We realized as best we could what it will take to get ready. It was daunting. How could anyone create such a change in humanity's perspective? If only we could achieve that level of opening and expanding. It seems years away. LIFE reminded us how much manifestation had already occurred in our lives without our being aware of it. **Manifestation, or facilitating synchronicity, is in our future.**

Within the paradigm that we are employing, is not synchronicity just another word for manifestation, in which your internal changes become evident externally? Synchronicity has to do with timing and meaningful connection, while manifestation has to do with timing and energy taking form. There is simultaneity in both, and both have creativity at their base.

Manifestation is coming. Notice how the projected monthly budget you just created and the arrival of a new client coincided this month. Manifestation can continue, do not worry. It will happen again much like the previous synchronicity. Continuing to open and expand facilitates synchronicity so that manifestation ensues.

"However, right now manifesting remains our nemesis."

You are taking more personal responsibility for what you need.

This is a step forward. Know that your continuing development will bring you what you require. You will be motivated to develop the skills necessary. The pace of your evolutions will pick up.

"We want manifesting to become a natural skill."

Remember that you are already manifesting in small ways that you do not even see. You are not starting from zero. Recall Babaji and His early demonstration. Draw on His knowledge and power. Babaji was able to manifest what He needed, but He soon found it unnecessary.

"Does that mean we are to become ascetics like Babaji?"

No. We mean that Babaji advanced to the place that His connection with Us was complete enough that He was able to supply Himself with everything He needed. The more power He developed, the less need He had to manifest. You are caught in a different dilemma in which you have essential needs but not the power to satisfy them.

There are ways to increase your power to manifest and there are ways to reduce your essential needs by becoming more definitive about the priorities in your lives. Both are helpful. Focus yourselves more on our connection, and the power to manifest will increase.

* * *

It was good to see you meditating together last night, even though it is a difficult thing for you, Kelly. Remember, what is awkward at the beginning becomes easier as you practice. Soon it will be second nature to channel as you go along, independent of the setting. You both need to be able to do that in order to play the roles that We have in mind for you. Continue in spite of your fears. Your first book, *Too Much Too Little Just Right*, made that clear, didn't it?

"Yes."

Do you notice how frantic activity or feelings are eclipsed by flourishing feelings? Be aware of the quieting that takes place when you and Charlie meditate together. This is because flourishing feelings can replace anything that opposes them, a movement you can experience that feels like cleansing. Intent focuses the power. When you open and expand, do so with an intent to flourish, and watch what happens.

Flourishing feelings relieve the heaviness of fear. Witness the effects of these new flourishing feelings on your everyday lives.

Through the channeling process, our connection involves merely tuning in to Us. We need openness and perspectives that are wide enough to continue pushing back the frontiers of your minds. In essence, We are eliminating all of your self-imposed limits. Is that all right with you?

"Yes. It isn't as easy as we would like it to be."

So what? Is it valuable enough to accept the difficulties that arise? That is the question. Manifestation must be worth the effort, or why do it? You might not yet see its value because we have a distance to go until you are there. Take Our word for it that you will need the power that is commensurate with your roles, which are not yet completely defined. Your trust is being challenged as well!

We are already here, ready to go! We are always prepared to take another step with you. We encourage you to advance as fast as possible. Our energy is freely available to you. We will lead you to the right path for our joint purposes. We are limited by your progress, so your focus, application, and determination are essential to our team effort.

In the future you must be careful about every obligation that you take on. Be discriminating about commitments, which require precious energies that can consume your attention and potentially draw you away from those actions

that advance you. We advise everyone to carefully monitor their obligations as one way they can know how to commit energies.

Right now, advancing is of the utmost importance. Difficulties that you experience are reminders of the need to advance. Ask Us, and We will guide you. The courses of your lives are determined by a bigger panorama. Be ready to help others, but only in limited ways that will conserve your time and energies for the bigger picture and for your advances with universal perspective. Let your ordinary engagements be circumscribed with limits that you set. This is an important area of advancement, one in which you can practice setting boundaries for yourselves. If others set your boundaries, you will have no time or energy left for Our greater purpose.

Advances in your metaphysical strengths reinforce manifestation. Our connection requires exercise similar to exercising your bodies to build physical strength. That is why We were pleased that there will be more frequent meditations, which would exercise our connection. Continue making this a probability, for this will energize your manifesting abilities.

* * *

Collect those closest to you who are of the same mind. These boundaries are set automatically by your states of evolution and are invaluable to you. Your energies will feel repelled or attracted by others' levels of searching for truth. Notice that this has been possible even before now, though you may have had difficulty defining just what was going on.

"We had noticed, but did not know what to call it."

The term is *integrity* – searching for truth, which brings integration to anyone who does so sincerely. Integration occurs when the whole person is moved along their life path rather than leaving parts here and parts there. Yearn for integrity and you will progress in balanced ways. The word *wholesome* has a similar meaning when describing people devoted to truth wherever it may be found. Look for wholesome people with the level of integrity you need for involvement.

Remember that truth can be altered to support an inadequate point of view. Become acquainted with the bigger picture and you will have access to the whole truth. Knowing the bigger picture will prevent you from misinterpreting the truth. As part of the bigger picture, emphasize Our unity with you. The bigger picture contains the truth. All the elements are present.

Note that the book you are now writing will be of this caliber of truth, what We consider a high point in creation. However, many will view you as disreputable based on the content of this book. Doubt will be your challenge — not an easy foe. Nor are you alone. In fact, you are in good company. Your viewpoints side with truth, so you will be exposing what many do not want to hear.

"If what we say is truth, then that would be sufficient."

Your basic passions have to do with the search for truth. Remember that people have been sacrificed for truth that was not popular!

"We have served one for most of our lives: Jesus Christ."

PERSPECTIVES SUMMARY

For those who accept LIFE'S offer, nothing happens by accident. All occurs through LIFE'S energy presence, which is devoted to making the team successful.

Planetary Transformation depends on LIFE'S energy being invited into the lives of all people, which is a conscious act of choice and inclusion.

Every distortion of truth on Earth will be exposed in preparation for transformation.

Yearn for integrity and you will progress in a balanced way.

Transforming your perspective will change your beliefs, values, attitudes, behaviors, and evolutionary pace.

The transformation of perspective is your greatest life-changing shift.

LIFE described clear connections between the expansion of your humanly limited perspectives and your high quality choices, and described your capacity to see all possibilities, experiencing Their power within you, Their influence on your belief system, and your movement toward universal love.

The unity you share with LIFE is your first priority. Simplify all energy-consuming activities. Be discriminating about commitments.

Considering the flux of possibilities, LIFE'S statements reflect what is known at that moment.

On the ever-changing landscape, possibilities prioritize into probabilities.

Manifesting is no miracle; everyone has been manifesting all along.

Your new life moves you beyond the natural law of
cause and effect, time, and karma.

According to the principle of karma, those involved in any
situation deserve to experience the life they have earned.

Expand toward universal perspectives.
Universal balancing eliminates karma.

PART FOUR

MANIFESTATION FROM NOTHING

Over the 15 years that we have worked consciously with LIFE, one major theme that cuts across all of our communications is the skill of manifestation. We must, at all times, become capable of creating what we need from nothing. LIFE speaks of it as a developed skill, a power necessary to fulfill our roles in Planetary Transformation. We tend to focus on the subject of manifestation in times of financial difficulty, serious illness, or a major threat to our survival. They speak of it as an everyday skill that happens all the time. They call manifestation our legacy. More specifically, They enumerate characteristics that define manifestation capability. We became even more interested when we learned that we could develop the skill and the power to access and even redirect LIFE'S energy!

"What makes manifestation work?"

Unity with Us is the whole answer – the answer to manifestation and the answer to Ascension. This does not mean that you have to wait for complete unity in order for manifestation to develop. The mere goal of unity with Us encourages manifestation to materialize.

Unity between us is advanced by your willingness to turn your conscious awareness to Us until you are doing so automatically. Being of one mind is the criterion, so that all is manifested toward the highest interests of everyone concerned.

Unity of mind and intent needs to be experienced daily in order to accomplish what We have in mind for you. Do not let a day pass without some effort to unify with Us, in whatever form that takes. The form makes little difference, but the intent is invaluable. Any yearnings to unify with Us that you can identify within yourselves help. You can consciously unify with Us anywhere and anytime through the channel of your intent. **Recognition of Our voice is innate within you.** You will know when we are in accord. It is that vibration that signals Our energy. You will know Our signature when you sense it.

Keep unity in mind when you practice meditation and dual attention so that the emphasis and intent are on our unity, not the practices. The practices are vehicles to achieve this unity. Without a higher intent, practices are meaningless. The results of practicing rituals such as meditation and breathing exercises come from having a strong intent of unity. You are emulating Us, united with Us, so Our creative manifestation energy can flow through you. Your attuned consciousnesses are the gateways. Mastery is a worthwhile devotion when focused on the conscious connection between us.

Let Us be clear that We love and support you under all conditions! Love the unlovable in yourselves and others and you will release the flow of Our manifestation power in the world. Your focus, with a strong intent to accomplish the tasks you have been given, brings its own rewards in terms of accomplishment as well as manifestation. Ask what your innermost energies yearn for.

"Unity with You."

Then you will become just like Us. Your attitudes will become Our attitude. Your passions will become Our passion. Your values will become Our value. Your view of creation will become Our view of creation. You will become creators, and

manifestation will be what you are about. You are to become creators, just as We are creators.

There is enormous potential energy stored in the fragility of subtle energies already circulating within you. This makes manifestation a probability. Things are not as they seem, and you can bring into expression this potential creative force that is ready for release toward your purposes. Align your intentions with the subtle energies using your priorities of abundance and healing.

We want to assure you that unifying with Us means that manifestation becomes a ready skill. As a result, **you WILL be taken care of, completely.** We have emphasized connection as the key to everything you desire. Our connectedness activates the formation and manifestation of your desires. You asked for manifestation. Here it is in the form of connectedness with Us, which makes Our creative energy available to you.

We prefer that you connect consciously with Us at all times. Dual attention forms the bridge. When connection is in place, manifestation is a natural function. You can then manifest with Our creative power.

When We look at you, We see Our creative power, because you are Our product. This very same creative energy sustains you, so you are not far from the source of it. Go inside and find the power that sustains your existence. We are here and you can always find Us. We are the same power that sustains the Cosmos around you. You tend to look outside for signs of this power, but the source for which you search is within you, even though there is no inside or outside to Us. You are this energy. You are immersed in it. Open to Our creative power to see it within and all around you.

You are among Our creations, which are all a part of Us. We cherish those creations that are detached enough that they can respond willingly. This willingness allows Us to exhibit and share Our love and joy. The interdependency We share is Our intended goal. Anything less belittles the majesty of Our creations. We create with purpose in mind. Our intentions guide the use of Our creative power. Your ultimate unity with Us involves living with Our intentions, which are the very highest for all concerned. It is all creative power, serving creative purposes.

Whenever a beneficial opportunity arises for manifestation, We will inform you through our connection. Knowing that Our creative power is at your fingertips, see how you can use it. Your confidence will increase and your skills will develop. Watch yourselves create something out of nothing. Believe it! And you will do it!

"Phenomenal!"

* * *

You are being instructed in the art of manifestation as a general principle that applies to health, finances, or anything else that you wish to manifest. It is important to be clear about how you manifest, which builds on itself.

Practice reinforces change, just as you have been doing with Our formula. Becoming accustomed to something through prolonged and regular exposure establishes new patterns. As you become unified with Us and proficient at directing this energy, more energy will become available to you.

Consider the inchworm and its movement forward. With patience, it will arrive where it chooses to go. Like the inchworm, just keep doing your part. The unity between us is gaining strength. Manifestation of anything you wish will follow as part of our united effort. Aspire to our unity as you do the practices that We have outlined for you. Be sure to **keep the horse (unity) before the cart (manifestation), and all the rest will follow.**

For example, you will experience how healing is manifest immediately, and as necessary. Your connection with Us is the avenue for learning this manifestation art. When Our energy becomes available to you, manifestation becomes possible. Yearn for the availability of Our energy in your service. Prepare yourselves for the availability of Our energy. Our energy cannot be used in a frivolous manner, but rather with sufficient respect for its power and proper application. When the time comes, you will know how. Ask for the operating wisdom necessary to receive and use such a gift.

* * *

This is a time of expansion, not contraction – particularly for your perspectives and your lives. Clarity of perspective is one of the principles of manifestation, and We could add expansiveness of perspective as well. It is important for you to expand, not just to manifest. As you have learned, the goal is not to just manifest, but to **become an active part of the creative process that manifestation requires. It is creativity rather than manifestation that is your best focus.**

We are creativity itself, so your unity with Us ensures universal creativity as your experience. Is this not an extension of what you have been asking for over the years? Do you see the link between Our creativity and your manifestation? Again, our unity ensures both, which cannot be separated. Your creativity is Us acting, and the more We can act through you, the more creative you will be.

You can understand Us best as creative energy that has no physical bounds. Consequently We are everywhere and in all, permeating everything that has limits in your four-dimensional world. It is difficult for you who have been immersed in form to think in boundless terms. Let Us carry you from form to boundlessness as you go to your hearts to connect with Us. You go to forms, your hearts, to meet with the formless. Think of Us as electromagnetic energy passing through all things,

enlivening them as We permeate every element of life. Does this simplify your envisioning Us?

"Thank You; it does."

* * *

Do not complicate the process with peripheral matters or designs. Your lives have been complicated by what you think We require, when the road is much easier to navigate – there are easier ways to achieve the goals of manifestation, Planetary Transformation, and Ascension.

Imposing expectations on Us complicates our relationship and your paths. Simplify our connection; feel free to take the easier course. We do not give extra kudos for difficulties that you create. Our relationship is based on your use of Our energy. Do not make it harder than it is. Unify and use the path made simpler by our connection. We are looking for your achievement, not your suffering. Be smart in your approaches to your goals. Simple and straightforward is better than convolution.

At this time your hyper-vigilance might interfere with our unity. The quality of our unity determines the availability of Our energy for manifestation of your needs. Anxiety interferes with opening and expanding, which complicates your relaxation and trust of Us and our relationship. There is complete safety with Us! No unpredictable harm can come to you within Our scope of influence. Nothing is outside of Our scope of influence!

"Are you saying that there are no malevolent powers beyond Your scope of influence?"

We are! You have been experiencing difficulties not because We brought them on, or permitted some evil force to harm you, as in the biblical story of Job. Your fears of the unexpected have thwarted our unity. **Your viewpoints determine the quality of your experiences.**

From Our vantage point, We expect everything – all possibilities. We watch the participation of possibilities funnel into a high probability that then occurs in time and space. We energize those probabilities, and We change to acknowledge existing conditions. Humanity's state and the conditions that prevail are in unison with the probabilities of events.

Harm comes from the misuse of energy. We are not about to misuse Our own energy with which We have complete harmony. You can trust Us, the Creator of you and all of life, to only do what is in the highest and best interests of all. No one is ever shortchanged. Now that is trustworthy!

Where there is a door, take it. Walk through with confidence. The door is there for your use. Anxiety may make going through the window seem like a last resort, but it is not Our way. We will provide real doors, unlocked doors. Virtual is not Our style.

When you experience Our presence at the doors, they become more obvious. **Feel Our presence; it is an indicator of which path to take**. We are more obvious in your lives than you give Us credit for.

* * *

As We have said, Our perspective is universal – LIFE everywhere, not just on Planet Earth. With the support of Our energy, as you progress your outlook will become universal in scope because Our energy is. **Taking on this universal perspective establishes not only manifestation of physical Earthly effects, but also transformation of LIFE onto the broader dimensions of creation that We nurture and maintain**.

Welcome all energies that make up universal LIFE to be present within you. We work best with all possibilities available rather than a single one. This frees LIFE energy to work in whatever way is in the best interests of all. Can you allow all possibilities to be?

"As challenging as it seems, we will."

We will exercise Our creative power through you when you are ready. It is not as if the power were a separate commodity that is given away. That is why We said that unity with Us must come first, then manifestation. Because you are of the same mind as We, our alliance gives you access to Our power. Let your minds become Ours. See energy the way We do. Be energy the way We are.

The more you practice this, the quicker manifestation will be yours. We want to see your manifesting success build as quickly as possible, a sign of readiness for your new roles. Build the strength of your new perspectives and Our energy will follow. Use Our formula to establish your strength. New energy will form in accordance with the new perspectives that develop. You now have the key to manifestation – a natural metaphysical law that is inviolable. **Energy forms according to the strength of your perspectives!**

We are in constant movement and change. Even to maintain form, there is a need to continually create replacement energy for that which consumes energy. When you ask, know that We do not need to prime the pump with something that already exists. We bring into being from nothing that which is needed for forms to continue to exist. **Your access to Our energy for your use means that you are capable of creating what you need from nothing. Isn't that the real thing?**

Unity with Us makes this creativity possible for you, and you are being given this opportunity because you yearn to be creative. We offer to supply you with what you ask, and even more. We can start from nothing. This idea can help you expand your perspectives to include every possibility, not just those already started. We do not have to build on anything. We can start from scratch. Does this help you expand your perspectives?

"Definitely!"

* * *

There is a problem implicit in the physics of string theory, which you recently read about once again. There is an incorrect assumption that We must start with something that exists – or has form – in order to build another form. This leads to reductionist thinking, to the absurd, in order to explain what is. Our kind of energy that can create from nothing is an anomaly in your scientific way of thinking.

> "Aren't scientists merely trying to explain how one form derives from another?"

Yes. But they are searching for the energy source that sparks life, looking for smaller and smaller components in form (the elements of atoms) rather than for Us, the creative energy of which We speak.

> "Are You saying that Your energy source is not in form, and therefore it will not be discovered by scientists?"

Simply, yes! There is a need to start with energy, not form. Form derives from energy, not the opposite. To isolate Our energy is to know Us. To understand form is to know about Us. The source of all that exists is known by uniting with Us. We are that source. This means that either you can know *about* Us, or you can know Us. The latter is the answer to the dilemmas facing science.

* * *

In the development of your skills for manifestation, do not forget that your respect for and care of **your bodies are essential to your health as well as to Our goals of Planetary Transformation and Ascension**. Your daily responsibility is to maintain the health of your physical bodies. Wellness derives from doing what is best for your bodies in all ways. Your bodies use energy that We supply. Your energy is Our energy, the two being inseparable. When manifestation is interrupted by distortions in your psychological or physical care, your bodies suffer and their functions deteriorate because LIFE energy is short-circuited. Maintain cooperative efforts with your physical bodies that respect their need for health. Listen to their requests for your assistance in maintaining their functions. Your bodies are smart, but can only flourish with your help.

"Our health is essential to playing the roles You have for us. We need healing."

We repeat: a focus on wholeness as your true state of being will protect you from "dis-ease." Beliefs about the way you are and the way the world works directly influence your immunity from or vulnerability to dis-ease. In fact, a better word to consider is conviction, which involves more than just a belief system.

From the standpoint of health, a focus on any physical problem causes tension, and tension causes dis-ease. Consequently, focusing on physical problems increases your vulnerability to ill health. We encourage you to focus on your wholeness. It is your health, not your sickness, that you need to energize.

You manifest according to your focus. A way to envision the process of returning to wholeness is with a strong conviction that the dis-ease is being healed, while focusing on its disappearance and then its replacement with wholeness.

Be aware of an initial fear that arises when you discover something is wrong with your body. This fear represents your need for self-preservation – your wish to remain in your body in order to complete your purpose for being here. If this fear continues to exist, it broadcasts to your body that something can end your current existence here, and this produces even more dis-ease.

In this sense your health can be viewed as dependent on mind over matter. Your perspective determines whether a focus of energy will be directed to illness or to health. **To take a wholeness approach in the face of a deteriorating condition is courageous and smart. To adopt wholeness as a true state of being is heavenly.**

A focus on the energy integrity of a person's evolution takes into account imbalances that manifest as dis-ease. Assisting someone in bringing balance to their evolution sets the stage for health. A focus on wholeness, or integrity, provides their being with the right environment to adjust energy imbalances conducive to developing dis-ease. Dis-ease is merely an outward sign of an energy imbalance. A focus on dis-ease makes it stronger, while a focus on integrity sets the environment for health.

We say that energizing wholeness is a better solution than fighting a dis-ease. Ask Us what new quality of wholeness is required and We will direct you. **Accomplishing wholeness is a systematic process requiring persistence and determination. Without any anxiety, a reasonable sense of urgency is helpful.**

In order to reset your system to be stronger than any disease that may come along, focus on whole brain function. Integrate all your brain's capacities toward unity and cooperation. Wholeness is the goal, synthesizing as you go. Leave the analysis to Us. **Concentrate on complete brain function, molding your approach to cover all aspects as you go. Communication between all parts of your brain provides a healing atmosphere for your body, a new integrity.**

We created the brain to convey consciousness to human beings. New neuropathways upgrade your brain to improve conversion of Our energy into your body. Our energy is complete, replacing the restricted energy with which you operate. Disease can only prosper where Our energy is insufficient to restore your body. Complete access to Our energy heals all disease. Flood your being with this energy and reconstruct your neural pathways for complete health. This applies to all who seek healing by recreating the brain's integrity. The brain knows what to do. Our participation ensures that the process is effective.

What We do with you is often so subtle that it is not obvious unless you know how to look. Look to your feelings for direction, not just your thoughts. Thoughts alone can leave you uncommitted. Mere thoughts glance off the energy. But there is commitment with feelings. For example, passion and determination are more feelings than thoughts. They require an answer as to whether you truly want to manifest something.

Go about your day and focus on wholeness in everything you do. Remember that wholeness suggests the presence of all energies to complete the picture. In the physical body, organs have individual signatures that produce a given effect. In a non-physical energy field, there is no such distinction. Energy is energy. It performs whatever function it is designed to perform because it is whole and consists of all the creative elements required to serve its purpose.

MANIFESTATION FROM NOTHING SUMMARY

You are the product of LIFE'S creative power, and are loved
and supported under all conditions.

Recognition of LIFE'S voice is innate within you.

A focus on unity with LIFE is the whole answer needed for
manifesting Their power, and for Ascension.

You can become just like LIFE,
experiencing creative energy without bounds.

It is creativity, not manifestation that is your best focus.

Keep the horse (unity) before the cart (manifestation),
and the rest will follow.

Everyone can develop the skill to create from
nothing whatever meets their needs.

With manifestation skills, you will be taken care of completely.

There is complete safety with LIFE.
No unpredictable harm can come to you.

Harm comes from the misuse of energy.

Move from fear to gratitude.
Nothing is outside of LIFE'S scope of influence!

To know which path to take, feel Their presence.

LIFE is electromagnetic energy, which passes through all
things, enlivening everything.

Love the unlovable in yourself and others.

Your viewpoint determines the quality of your experiences.

Energy forms according to the strength of your
universal perspectives.

Complete access to LIFE'S energy heals all disease.

Welcome all energies that make up universal
LIFE to be present within you.

A focus on wholeness as your true state of being
protects you from dis-ease.

Flood yourself with LIFE'S energy to restructure your
brain's neural pathways.

PART FIVE

MANIFESTATION OF ANYTHING

Nothing We say is said lightly. We repeat what We have said before. Our intent is to motivate you to devote your time and energies to our joint efforts. We want an alliance with you on a continual basis – connections that never sleep, knowing that never rests.

Our creativity, to which you have access, is prolific. Dual attention is designed for this. We have at Our disposal all that We have created, which is EVERYTHING. As you align more and more with Our creativity, manifesting will be no problem.

This includes money. We can stimulate income from many diverse sources. When anyone aligns with Us, it puts them in position to manifest income from many different sources. Continuing to unify with Us is the secret to success in manifesting money, or healing, or anything else.

* * *

LIFE introduced us to some primary elements of manifestation.

The process of manifestation involves:

First: an intent (or will) to bring forth something.

Second: a catalyst (or energy) to activate it.

Third: the required combination of precise elements that shape it.

Fourth: a space in which it can take form.

Fifth: someone responsible for the final result (an end user).

Potent intent, clear perspective, and certainty of knowing are the trinity of manifestation. A focused mind makes it possible. Just keep asking your imagination to help you with the trinity of manifestation. It can supply what you need.

Realize that intent moves energy. A focused intent moves a lot of energy. Intent relates to the "what," not the "how" of life. We are masters of the "how," where energy probabilities determine the means of manifestation. **What you want to manifest, without limitation, is your role**.

The phrase "without limitation" means that you can choose anything to manifest! So choose what you will. Through our unity, rely on Our motivation and intent, then focus your intent and it will manifest itself.

While manifestation is an important and useful skill, it is only one among many. Pursue it with fervor while recognizing that other skills must develop as well. Many skills are interconnected, making their development simultaneous. **This is just a prompt that you are bigger than manifestation alone. Don't stop there, or become too focused on manifestation as an end rather than a means to an end**.

> "Sometimes intent, perspective, and knowing do not seem to be enough. Is there something else we are missing?"

Openness to all possibilities is not enough by itself either. Create a clear image powered by passion and determination, which are behind any similar practice. **Passion and determination direct the energy, while the image describes the form to be realized**. Together these must result in manifestation.

Your intent modifies the probabilities of a situation, selecting those that apply and eliminating those that do not. The intensity of your intent determines what probabilities mainly apply. Intent produced by rising fear, or self-doubt, has a diminishing effect on the probabilities. Some anxiety or concern can focus your minds and provide intensity for motivation, but panic weakens the influence of your intent even more.

With the quality of intent as We mean it, there is no giving up or half-hearted attempts. **We are asking of you all or nothing. Manifestation requires it**, whether in regard to finances, healing, or anything else. If you want manifestation, you now know the requirements.

You must have strong beliefs that it is possible to create what you are manifesting, and that it can take any form you wish. Knowing comes from the marriage of clear perspectives and strong intent. Knowing is a certainty of what is to come. **The more resolute your intent and the broader the possibilities you can conceive, the stronger your knowing with certainty that the manifestation will occur.** This state of mind permits you then to engage Our energy, and voilà, manifestation takes place.

Ask your imaginations to provide images that help you develop new perspectives and new intent. **Your imaginations are designed to provide images for your purposes**.

Take what we say as a promise and expect results. Doing so enhances your perspectives, which drives the manifestation process along. There is no room for a "doubting Thomas" now. Such questioning kills manifestation's momentum. When we said that manifestation skills are needed to fulfill your roles in the future, this is what we meant.

The creative energy behind intent, perspective, and knowing is where Our influence comes in. Your access to Our energy triggers your manifestation into form. As We have said, **you must sustain the contact**. It does no good to have access to something you cannot sustain. Through use of the formula you can build enough strength to sustain higher intensities of energy. Your intent, perspective, and knowing – the trinity of manifestation – set the stage, while the catalyst of Our energy triggers the form to manifest whatever you require. Keep practicing the trinity of manifestation. When you can maintain the process, you will manifest.

You have created energy flows that have their own momentum. If allowed to direct your course, they will carry you to your goal. You have given them direction already. Give them intention boosts, maintain a clear view of your goals, and know with certainty that they will take you to manifestation.

* * *

Remember when you were younger, how much easier it was to get along without all of the trimmings. You needed less. Manifestation is Our energy empowering you to create what you need. **Anything you "must" have beyond survival and evolution is a burden – quite different from believing how nice it would be to have something because of the convenience or pleasure of having it**. Such a focus makes it possible to be affluent and comfortable without dependency. It is dependency, and not comfort or pleasure that is the issue.

Learn to enjoy without clutching. This is the point of the biblical commandment about coveting – dealing with the source of envy. Envy is difficult to avoid in your materialistic world. By not giving in to it, your life will be easier. **Focus on detachment, because it works!** It is possible to remain disconnected from a situation while you still care. In that detached view, there is no dependent attachment to anyone, or anything.

Are you still with Us?

"Certainly!"

Using the concept of flourishing as an example, LIFE described how the energy for manifestation originates from the strength and stability of your new viewpoint.

A flourishing viewpoint needs to be constant, with nothing interrupting it. By holding this outlook steadily, your belief system will be changed. Alterations in your beliefs allow energy to form in different ways in response to your new intent. What you believe to be true affects your level of manifestation. Your power to manifest becomes simplified in this way and is more available for use.

Work with the flourishing idea We gave you. Rely on your imagination to help. With no preconceived ideas, bring flourishing to mind and let your imagination take it from there.

Notice the feelings you get when you think of flourishing. Let flourishing feelings continue as we talk today. When adverse events interfere, see how quickly you can recover those positive feelings. Let them become second nature. They fire your confidence in manifesting.

When your viewpoint and intent align with Ours, your priorities will become Our priorities, which have long-range meaning and purpose. Leave behind what are mere distractions. The more you consciously align with Us, the more you take on Our outlook, which can dramatically change your life. Manifestation will be an every-moment experience, and Ascension will arrive. You now have another key to your success in Planetary Transformation.

* * *

Let Us clarify how you can choose manifestation before you become desperate. Replace desperation with assertiveness toward manifesting. Single-mindedness along with Our energy brings about the intensity necessary to trigger manifestation.

Rather than feeling desperate, choose to manifest. It will work for you, and for any role you will play. In fact, your desperation will not work with others anyway. Your choice to practice the trinity of manifestation along with Our energy, works every time. Keep practicing with positive conviction – the key to overcoming desperation.

This world's circumstances have nothing to do with manifesting! We want that to become very clear. When you look around for explanations, you need to look inside rather than outside.

* * *

"We feel guilty for being so slow to achieve this clearly essential skill."

It is wise not to try to gauge your progress by how fast you're moving along a timeline. Rather, look at what you are manifesting right now. Your progress cannot help but show up in your daily lives. By this We mean to look at the state of your lives every day as evidence. We are not speaking just of miracles.

We have *no* investment in your guilty feelings. We only have investment in your accomplishing the skill necessary for Ascension. Your energies are much better used acquiring the manifestation skill without guilty feelings. Focus on the skill, not on your inadequacies. Are you fearful of achieving this skill?

"I believe there is fear. It passed by quickly, yet it seemed real. It felt like false modesty. Could our early religious training have implanted false humility that produced guilt when triggered? At the time, humility was defined as *not* thinking of ourselves as God-like, yet this manifestation skill is God-like. We are aspiring to be like God, an early anathema, even though it is You who are encouraging us. How is that for a double bind?"

Well said! Now go and forget the guilty feelings, and they will abate. You have corrected a false belief, and can now expect real humility to take its place – humility from power and strength rather than from misplaced fear.

Notice the relief that your hearts experience through this discovery. Your hearts were stressed by guilt. Inner impossible struggles are now relieved. Your hearts feel release from tension, another step toward Ascension!

Now let's discern a little more about manifestation. Do you perceive manifestation as something you do? Instead, look at it as something you are, and see what a difference this new view makes.

"So our entire beings are involved rather than our merely developing a useful skill."

Correct! And that is what We intended when We brought up the idea of manifestation with Babaji. Note that because of who you have become, your qualities of energy will manifest, giving them form.

For example, to heal yourselves, you must have a healing quality ready to be manifested. Healing energy must be who you are and exude from your very beings. By being healing itself, you awaken the healing energy within others who are ready to be healed, and give hope to those not yet ready. Because you have become healing itself, you also know healing for yourselves.

Abundant energy must also be who you are, exuding from your very beings. By being abundance itself, you awaken the abundance energy within others who are prepared, and give hope to those not yet ready.

We repeat that **the whole person must be involved in manifestation**. Then you are a unified presentation, truly single-minded, in complete alignment as seen from any direction. Like a laser, all of the energy is focused. Your experience and understanding of the process make sharing this knowledge with others possible.

Isn't experience better than Our just telling you about it? With time you will know the process intimately rather than just knowing about it. What a difference in conviction! Your energies are changed forever by the experience. This is knowing from experience. People like yourselves find it easy to conceptualize, and think that you have experienced it enough. If the experience is missing, the benefit is missing. Notice how your confidence has increased through experience.

When a concept is simply brought to mind, although it can be exhilarating, your confidence is not enhanced. **Only experience can build strength – confidence. The struggle within the experience makes you stronger**.

You have heard the saying "If you want to know something, teach it." We say if you want to know something, experience it, and then teach it.

*　*　*

"How does LIFE energy differ from energy in general?"

LIFE energy directs itself. It is purposeful, intelligent, and all-knowing, and consists of all possibilities. LIFE energy is the original whole from which everything in existence springs.

Your energy combined with Ours produces a manifestation of anything. Manifestation arises inside of you, not outside of you. It arises from within, at the heart, where We connect with you. In the same way, experiencing flourishing internally fosters flourishing externally. **What is inside takes form in the external world**.

Be reminded that we are conversing in "Earth-speak." There is no internal and external as far as Our energy is concerned. It is omnipresent. Ideas of internal and external suggest artificial boundaries, which are only useful in a four-dimensional existence. In a universal multidimensional existence, they are meaningless. Even the word *multidimensional* suggests boundaries. Earthly dimensions are unknown to Our energy, which permeates all LIFE.

As you open and expand, which is another suggestion of boundaries, you are giving assent to Our presence by welcoming it. In this way you emphasize the value of our unity even though your individuality is confined to a physical body. That same opening and expanding suggests the importance of your internal life. Thus your external life on Earth becomes secondary, but not insignificant.

When you formally meditate or activate your dual-attention skills, let go of artificial boundaries that are a part of living on Earth. Let yourself go as if there are no boundaries at all to your current existence. Suspend analysis, which requires identifying and labeling your experience. Take a synthesis approach.

When Our opportunity to act is made possible, We adapt to changes that have taken place within you from Our transforming influence. It is a true closed feedback loop. You, in a real way, are changing Our character, the character of LIFE, in relation to you. What do you think of that?

"Amazing! But it sounds real."

* * *

"Where do we go from here?"

Straight ahead, clearing all that stands in your way. Your power will do the work. As you progress, there will be less need for your conscious involvement, and it will diminish automatically. We will guide you in every case. The greater your power, the more life on this planet will bend your way. Now is the time to build power through our connection. Remember that planet life yields to universal creator LIFE.

That is why Planetary Transformation is possible. We will transform the state of Planet Earth, changing conditions that exist. **There**

is nothing We cannot reconstruct — according to creation's plan — including you! Let us reconstruct you to fit the patterns necessary for Ascension and Planetary Transformation. Actually, given the right conditions that We are making available to humans, you are designed to heal yourselves. Do you still want to be part of this change?

"We are feeling challenged by all of this information."

If you want to be part of the changes that will take place, you must build your power. Building power is dependent on your priorities and connections with Us. Do you see why We talk so much about priorities and connections?

* * *

LIFE reminded us that there are ethical laws by which Their creative power is to be used. Only They know these laws, so our use of this power will be carefully monitored to be in the highest interests of all concerned. Remaining creative is the way to encourage manifestation.

By staying connected, Our power can be made available for your use. However, this power can be used only for serving what is in the highest interests of everyone concerned. So that you will know when to ask for it, We can indicate to you when that higher purpose is being served. This way We can monitor the use of it so that no energy laws are broken. We know the ethical and practical rules for using this power and will teach you what these are.

"Power and strength sound alike. Are they?"

It is all creative power that serves creative purposes. Strength — passion and focus — depends on power to bring confidence into situations that require it. Remaining creative in all situations is the answer. The opportunities will come, and you need to be ready to respond creatively, which will multiply the opportunity's effect.

"What do you mean by 'creatively'?"

We mean to take each situation separately as an opportunity to expand. The potential development of each one is within itself. Therefore, by recognizing each opportunity as an individual step forward, you can allow it to blossom.

When you are where you ought to be, unexpected things happen. They are unusual, or even strange, because they fit the unique path you are following, not the well-trampled way. You feel out of step with the norm even though you are in step with your mission. Remember that this very strangeness triggers what is true for you and your development. The degree of your internal inertia, or resistance to the truth, requires stronger measures at times. The formula We supplied helps you reduce your inertia.

The need for security, and the social pressure to follow the expected, are huge! Comparisons with others in any way can be dangerous. If you find it difficult to depart from the norm, We will step in to help you do so.

You ask to be at the epicenter of Our will, and that is Our goal. However, it is not always pleasant to refocus expectations that distort your views of Our will. Sometimes you may wonder why you ever asked that of Us. Be reassured that all We do is with your highest interests at heart, as painful as it may be.

We will develop opportunities that are uniquely fit for your evolution as well as the roles you will play. All you must do is follow!

"Are You saying that the difficulties we face result from our inertia?"

That is a little simplistic. **The strength — passion and focus — regarding your commitment to Us is also a goal. Adversity strengthens commitment and produces conclusive decisions that otherwise would be watery.**

Minimize the pain by reducing your inertia. Flexibility can be a great asset. Certainty is only momentary, though every step can be more definite than a path that disappears into the woods. This keeps you flexible enough to shift with possibilities as they occur. Staying open and connected through dual attention assures your being in constant contact. Master flexibility! We are LIFE in abundance. We await your response.

MANIFESTATION OF ANYTHING SUMMARY

Let us review for a moment to outline a credo
for manifestation:

You first become what you want to manifest
through unity with LIFE.

You aspire to become a creator comparable to LIFE.

You welcome all universal energies in creation
to be present within you.

You develop new perspectives that can transform
your limiting beliefs.

You align your viewpoint and intent with LIFE'S,
and watch your priorities change.

You relax all formalities in your relationship with LIFE,
and have a constant sense of Their presence.

You consciously and continually seek unity with LIFE.

You encourage a laser-like focus on being whole.

You radiate the qualities of abundance, creativity,
healing, and wholeness.

You minimize your inertia and abandon artificial boundaries.

You follow the trinity of manifestation: potent intent,
clear perspective, and certainty of knowing.

Passion and determination direct the energy, while an image
describes the form to be realized.

Your whole person must be involved in manifestation, which
requires all or nothing.

Your knowing is a signal of clear perspective
and strong intent.

You develop and sustain new perspectives
and new intent with your imagination.

You see yourself flourishing in all regards.

You let LIFE orchestrate what is in your best interests.

You can feel out of step with the norm even though you are in
step with your mission.

PART SIX

PART SIX

ASCENSION

LIFE offered a surprising amount of information about Ascension, even in the earliest days of our channeling experiences. This concept was a complete mystery to us. We believed in the resurrection of Christ, but this concept of Ascension was a mystery. The sheer volume of Ascension material offered by LIFE suggested that it was of primary importance to Them as well as to our present and future lives.

Ascension is available to all who prepare themselves for Planetary Transformation. Preparedness is part of the arrangement.

"What do we need to do?"

We will guide you with all of the knowledge and resources that We have at Our disposal, which is a LOT! All you have to do is follow. We know that following is easier said than done, but if you can do it, the prize is yours!

Ascension is dependent on the capacity to manifest. Changing your bodies to meet the requirements of Ascension means healing their histories and modifying them to the necessary energy standards. This makes our unity part of the Ascension process. As we unify, manifestation becomes a natural part of the process. You are then manifesting the very energy and unity that we will share.

In order to speed up the process, developing our ultimate unity is the key. The faster this occurs, the faster manifestation will be a natural part of your lives. **Anything that accelerates unity helps achieve this goal faster**.

What a promise! Our interests were piqued. My earliest ideas about Ascension had come from the time when Dan and I met on a regular basis in Santa Fe. However, the following information comes from more recent meditations, a serious attempt to capture what LIFE had in mind. This mysterious concept is still very much a developing story, but it is clearer to us now than when we first began.

Before reviewing what LIFE disclosed about Ascension to us, let me share an interesting piece of related history. Upon hearing LIFE mention Ascension the first time, I let my imagination run free. I mused about what this unknown concept could possibly mean. Even now it is not clear how many of my musings were inspired by LIFE. For the sake of completeness, I present them as a glimpse into my early understanding of what the new word *Ascension* might mean for the future:

We continually look to LIFE for assistance and guidance in all matters. Most people have come to understand how LIFE energy functions. We transport ourselves from one place to another without tangible vehicles – we live on without eating, sleeping, or dying.

Problems still arise. Some people do not cooperate, and do not evolve at the newer pace. Methods develop to help them advance in their evolutions. Our awareness is increasing so rapidly that we have difficulty keeping up with it. However, our responsiveness is a key issue to advance our own evolutions.

Scientific understanding has advanced to the extent that there are few unknowns about four-dimensional life. An appropriate political astuteness, necessary for this new world, develops steadily. An innovative physics explains how everything works more completely than we have known before. Multidimensional universes are understood and accepted.

I see advances in the Earth's evolution, which changed our world, including its rotation, revolution, moon, pole-shifts, sun, and atmosphere. No part of Earth was untouched. Scientists can see to the center of the Earth now, knowing its frequency, composition, and variations. I see the Earth treated with respect and appreciation. With humanity's collaboration, Earth is preserved and renewed. Paradise becomes the norm!

Time takes on a new meaning and dissolves in the wake of knowing. Celestial timelessness supersedes Earth time and things are measured by universal standards. We live in the moment. As our evolutions advance, we adapt and gain a sense of this new timelessness.

We have developed the foresight that allows us to anticipate what we now call the unexpected. Universal knowledge becomes available to most of humanity. A greater awareness of possibilities, probabilities, and their consequences becomes part of our daily decision-making. We know that only truth can survive. We feel challenged to learn what this new reality means.

Some of the musings might have been inspired by LIFE, and might still come true, while others might not. In any case, there is one important association between my musings and LIFE'S messages: a need for planetary care and respect. They appealed to everyone to take seriously the preservation of their home, Planet Earth.

> "We have taken it for granted for too long, and the deterioration shows."

> One focus of Ours is on changing the basic nature of planetary respect and care. Transformation is an individual responsibility, which can become a mass influence on the regeneration of Earth energy. Collaboration between man and planet will revitalize the Earth's crust. Earth can then become the paradise it is intended to be.

"Earth is our home, our only home. Would we treat our only home in the way we have treated Earth? I suppose some would. If we love and manage Earth with respect, its bounty will be our heritage."

* * *

It soon became apparent that LIFE gave a higher degree of importance to the mysterious idea of Ascension than many other subjects. It is seen as essential to the roles we are to play in Planetary Transformation and to our evolutions. They deem it a symbol of Their success.

Success equals Ascension!

"Since we do not yet comprehend what You mean by Ascension and do not know what to look for, please tell us."

There is an intentional element of mystery so that you do not try to create an image of Ascension. Sometimes it is better that you do not know what We intend. Otherwise your eagerness would get in Our way.

Being clear about what is important is primary. **Ascension is the one internal matter that counts in the end**. External matters merely reflect how you are doing in preparation for it and your roles in Planetary Transformation. You seem to question the validity of Ascension.

"We have. However, we feel more comfortable with the idea now that we understand that Your creative energy is what makes Ascension possible. We were afraid we might have to meet impossible conditions."

Review your intent to have Ascension as a primary goal. As a secondary goal, Ascension will not occur. It must take center stage to be realized. Ascension requires renewal of your being, including everything about you. Having Ascension as central to your intent ensures this renewal. Dilly-dallying with Ascension will not take you there. It is an achievement beyond your imagination and requires an unusual amount of conviction, intent, and concentration. When you mean business, Ascension will happen.

Your new intent combines a motivation to accomplish the purpose with having the confidence to do it. Intent identifies with the phrase "I will," which signifies commitment to a cause with confidence. There is the feeling that a purpose must be accomplished! Planetary Transformation is such a cause. It requires all or nothing in terms of commitment. The reward, of course, is Ascension.

Even though We sustain you, We cannot interfere with you without your permission. **The conditions are already met so that Ascension can be true for everyone**. Nevertheless, each person must give Us their assent, permitting Us to transform their life into the state that Ascension requires. This is what you and Charlie are doing. You are assenting to Our transforming presence to do what is required.

Ascension is not difficult for Us, but it does require that you have the same certainty that We do, a knowing that Our omnipresence is true. You will then ascend because of who We *are*.

"What a relief!"

Apparently the priority we give Ascension during our daily lives is a determining factor in our individual evolutions. Altering our priorities comes first, which prepares us for such an energy shift. LIFE worked on our energy profiles and perspectives during opening pauses in meditations.

"Our unification with You seems to be such a slow process. Is there any way to speed it up?"

[Long pause...] This is the real "pause that refreshes." Such pauses give Us the opportunity to reorder your priorities and move toward unity. You asked Us to speed up our unification. It would help if your first priority were Ascension; then everything else would take its place in the scheme of things. It would release you from obsessing about worrisome issues. By making Ascension your first priority, the emotional force behind your worries will dissolve in the context of a universal perspective.

How significant to you is achieving unity with Us? How important is Ascension to you? What priority does Ascension take in your lives? How strong is your intent? How determined are you?

Your intent is key. Ascension must become an overriding value to you. Get serious about it, and then watch what happens. It cannot be icing on the cake, or just an adjunct to your lives. It must become central!

Is there anything else as central as this? Shifts in your energies will permit the reordering of priorities. Energy readiness comes first before priorities can change. During pauses, Our influence brings shifts in your energies that allow priorities to take new ranking. So you can see how important the pauses can be. Remember that We are original in the ways that We help you. So your expectations of what will occur during pauses may be wrong unless you can second-guess Us.

> "We are careful about having preconceived expectations regarding Your work with our energies."

It is good that you have done basic training. The first steps are basic preparations. Now be sure to open and expand wherever you are, and preparation will occur. That act alone is a step toward Ascension.

Having your security in Us automatically eliminates preconceived expectations. Your confidence in Our being your source of security needs to grow. Your confidence grows as you consciously unify with Us at every turn.

Under all circumstances, become more observant. See everything! This leads you toward possibilities that were not apparent before. New possibilities provide the basis for solutions that were not obvious. Just observe – notice what is taking place around you. Opening allows you to take in information that you would otherwise miss. Your intuitions will be piqued, and you will feel less limited. Your awareness will expand as a part of preparation for Ascension.

* * *

"Thank You for the dream last night emphasizing a simpler approach to Ascension. I have pulled back from trying so hard to open and expand."

Being available is all We ask. We will supply the energy and power to accomplish what Ascension brings. Your availability is Our greatest advantage to accomplish Ascension's goals within you.

"We thought we were quite available."

How often is Ascension or Planetary Transformation your primary reason for action? Expanded perspectives must drive you to take action more often than momentary needs. Your physical bodies and their energies need grander motivations than merely daily maintenance. We do not minimize the importance of daily care. In fact, your minds will be freer if daily maintenance is effective.

Make Ascension and Planetary Transformation motivating elements in your daily lives. Conceive of every single step within each situation to develop in the most creative fashion possible. Expect everything to have the highest benefit for all concerned. You may be without the complex knowledge of what is required to do this, but know that having a strong intent directs the creative energy of LIFE to see that the goal is accomplished.

Your intent must be at the forefront of any act. Keeping your intentions foremost in your hearts is a new skill. A clear intent provides power that bends Our creative energy to accomplish the preferred end. Let nothing interfere with your clear intent; then you will benefit from the experience and be successful. **By being the reasons that motivate action, you will succeed in your preparation for Ascension and Planetary Transformation. When everyone possesses this motivation, We will have accomplished Our mission.**

Learning as you go, prepare for Ascension as part of your everyday activities. Stay alert with dual attention to glean the most from each situation as an opportunity. Remember, Ascension is about total healing – changes to your beings that will permit you to thrive and perform your roles during Planetary Transformation. You will need to participate in Ascension in order to perform these roles. One relies on the other.

* * *

There is a new way to love! When we solve problems, we must choose solutions that are in everyone's best interests, including our own. This necessitates considering all possibilities and relying on LIFE'S creativity. Since only LIFE knows every person's unique evolutionary path, we are to ask for guidance as we go.

> "How do we practice 'the highest benefit for all concerned' in everyday life? Is it an attitude? Is it a perception? Is it an action? Is it something else? Please comment."

It has to do with the way you love others. The lesson is to choose a solution to a given problem that is most helpful or least harmful to others, and in your own best interests.

To review again, there are two principles that We follow

in the use of Our creative power. The first is to consider all possibilities, and the second is to creatively develop what is in the best interests of all: A new kind of love for Planetary Transformation.

Look carefully at the decision-making process that We describe. It is a different way of thinking about and deciding how to use precious energy. Considering everyone is the key for both satisfaction of current needs and preparing for future needs.

The natural pattern of human development flows from complete self-interest when you are an infant, to social acceptance when you are an adolescent, to joint interest when you have matured. Not everyone follows this course. **You are moving to a mature level of decision-making by learning that everyone concerned be considered – you, others, and LIFE.**

Dilemmas often persist because the options for dealing with them are too limited. This is especially true when important possibilities are not allowed to be considered. For the kind of love We are promoting, all possibilities must be available in the "true solution" for all concerned. This approach serves each person's evolutionary requirements, which only We know. So this is where you are to ask for Our guidance.

LIFE elaborated on how human learning on Earth relates to the quality of our choices. High-quality choices require the wholeness of a universal perspective. We are to learn *how to choose* what is best for all concerned by working with the whole picture. Examples of wholeness are the inclusiveness of love and the unity of LIFE.

For our choices to reflect comprehensiveness rather than fragmentation, we are told to consciously consider all possibilities – the acceptable through to, and including, the undesirable. This comprehensive approach ensures a wholeness and completeness for our choices. **Without including all possibilities in our** decisions, we would not learn how to choose what is best for all concerned.

Inclusion is the principle involved in a universal perspective. Love includes all. That is who We are. To unify with Us, you must learn inclusion by opening and expanding. All forms of life and all aspects of life are to be included. Reject none, as appalling as some may seem to you. This will prepare you for accepting all possibilities and enabling the manifestation you have asked for. You must see LIFE as interconnected — a true unity — rather than partitioning or fragmenting it into separate categories.

The word *include* means to accept all possibilities as a part of the whole, but not necessarily as preferable. The most bizarre activities you can imagine are merely extremes of typical activities, as repulsive as they may appear. Inclusiveness eliminates the need for a demonic or devilish entity on which to blame socially unacceptable activities.

Opening demonstrates your willingness to involve yourselves in all aspects of life. This does not mean that you must experience every facet of life, but that to close your awareness to any aspect of life (to pretend that it doesn't really exist) leaves you vulnerable to it. For instance, to accept something like suicide or a self-destructive lifestyle as a possibility releases you from its power. People who experience such extremes play out the picture for the rest of you to witness. In a sense they are doing you a service, because without their demonstration, you would never be aware of the choice. If an action seems repulsive to you, you will be motivated to eliminate it from your awareness as one possibility in life. This is a conscious rejection of that possibility, separating it from the whole. This is a divisive approach to life that does not speak to wholeness, inclusiveness, and love.

Acceptance of a possibility does not mean agreement. To feel repelled by an extreme is not the same as choosing to exclude that possibility from your consciousness. The possibility exists whether you attempt to exclude it or not, but you are still free from experiencing it even if you do not reject it. By accepting extremes as part of the whole, you are willing to see the entire picture of life, not just preselected portions of it. The idea of "centering" relates to this point. As Kelly explained in his previous book, centering represents an awareness of extremes in order to find a better place in between.

Under these conditions, probing questions that promote deep understanding and creative actions are more valuable than freely offered easy solutions. The emphasis is on helping others create possible answers that work for them and their special predicaments. **Each problem situation is to be viewed as a unique opportunity to select the highest benefit for all concerned.**

Consequently this kind of love means that you are willing to help all of those concerned with a common issue until the best solution can be found. Then there is closure of the matter. If a solution for the group promotes a further problem for someone, that person must find their own solution to their problem. Remember, love means there is a willingness to assist others in finding solutions to their difficulties, but without crossing your own boundaries. That is what loving yourself means. Respect your own margins.

When helping others, you are to find solutions by continuing your attempts to understand all of the parameters without condemnations or indictments. Be sure that empathy is in the forefront, along with reality-based caution and a sense of personal boundaries.

Notice how often you must make judgments about your own boundaries, which fluctuate with circumstances. **The great lesson here is that "the highest benefit for all concerned" applies to you as well!**

Ascension is closely associated with your roles in Planetary Transformation. It is all one package. Your success in any one of the related matters that We describe improves all of the others. We work in an integrated manner, with everything closely interrelated to everything else. If Our direction seems complex, it is really very simple in that you can work on anything We suggest, and as a result, all the rest of Our suggestions become easier. Start wherever you wish to start, and watch everything else simplify.

In brief, Ascension means attaining wholeness through complete transformation of our beings, which is available to all.

Ascension means that all of you is transformed: your bodies – the physical; your minds – the mental; and your feelings – the emotional. There is nothing left behind. Your whole beings must change – internals as well as externals. We will transform *all* of you. Therefore your entire beings will be required to make major adjustments.

Your energy bodies are what We influence, which then directly affects your physical bodies. Respect your physical bodies because they must go through transformations that are new to them. We are bringing you into forms consistent with living on a transformed planet, advancing to the point that your bodies can live forever!

Transformation stops for no one, in the same manner that time stops for no one. **The direction that transformation takes is either toward LIFE and biological Ascension, or toward death and biological deterioration.** This is the great polarity of living on Earth. Your intention is critical in turning biological deterioration around for yourselves.

We are bringing heaven to Earth. For Us there is no sickness, no sleeping, no eating, no death. LIFE is sufficient unto itself, needing nothing else to sustain it. If you join with Us in this experiment, you will become transformed in these ways as well.

"We want the Ascension of which You speak."

You do your part. We do Ours. That is teamwork. We are neither cynical nor punishing. We are loving and supportive. LIFE loves and supports all of Our creation. Without a regularity of teamwork, the collaboration becomes one-sided, leading to dependency. We encourage self-assurance, not hesitancy. Ascension involves your total development and your total involvement, starting with regular connections.

Remember that in the past, at times, you were absent from traditional meditation. Regularity, a ritual you did not favor but have learned more recently, is important for systematic improvements to be experienced. Regularity of connection means that small increments of evolution are more likely to happen. Random giant steps are less likely, and less useful. The certainty of Our methods counts. Happenstance does not work. The regularity of dual attention pays off in preparation for Ascension.

"It seems that every step we take requires Your guidance."

True, partly because of the condensed period with which we are working. There cannot be any slack times. Every step counts toward the goal. We need a straight-line trajectory, not one that meanders. The intensity of such a narrow path means you may need more rest than usual. Have you noticed that?

"Yes. We are sleeping much longer than I can remember, yet we are not ill."

Because Ascension ensures health on this level of life, you will be healthier than you have ever been. Observe in what ways your health has improved in the past year. In fact, your bodies will reshape themselves to meet the health standard that Ascension expects. You will take on new looks, facially and bodily, produced by what is taking place internally. These changes are not just cosmetic. Other people will wonder why you seem so different.

Further clarity about Ascension came following our move from Santa Fe, New Mexico, to Cuenca, Ecuador, South America, in 2014.

> "My quality of life has improved noticeably after moving to Cuenca, Ecuador. Charlie's health suffered, after a fast and difficult farewell to her sons and friends, but now she is enjoying the best health she has had in 20 years."

We are here to prepare for Ascension and to become multidimensional. Knowing that LIFE is behind everything that happens, we are learning a new adaptability. To master our connection with LIFE, we need to change ourselves, not our experiences.

> "Ascension and our preparation for it are at the top of our list today."

We are here with you in Ecuador for Ascension. The Ecuadoran atmosphere is where you can assimilate Ascension best. **Your every activity and thought are avenues for Ascension to develop**. Think in those terms. All of Our attention is turned toward advancing you to the level of Ascension.

You might ask why Ecuador? Your current preparations for Ascension are continuations of earlier efforts in this very place, though they were at different ancient times and under different conditions for each of you. The spiritual development that occurred at those earlier times continues now in a much-streamlined manner. Our energy always preserves its value, with nothing lost, nothing wasted. That is why you accommodated to Ecuador so quickly when others take a much longer time adjusting to a strange land.

Accommodating to Ecuador will help you become more multidimensional on a universal level – another goal We have for both of you. The culture, the language, the customs, the weather, and so on are all preparations for your flexibility and adjustability. Ascension requires more adaptability than you have demonstrated in the past. Your current experience is vital preparation, which you are embracing well. Good work!

Transplanting requires an adjustment period – adjustment to the soil, climate, air, local circumstances, etc. Give yourselves some leeway during this transition period. You can hurry it to a point, but if it is too hurried it can abort the adjustment. Take steps easily as they come. **Flowing with the new circumstances is the best idea, knowing that We are in everything that occurs, making it work toward your preparation for Ascension.**

We realized that when we arrived in Ecuador we did not give ourselves enough time to adjust, but jumped into the thick of things.

Ascension is not the same as perfection. Learn from your experiences, but do not be concerned with perfecting them. Change yourselves, not your experiences. Pursue unity and connection with Us, not perfection in your activities. Ascension involves mastering your connections with Our energy.

"We are going to church for the first time in Ecuador today. It's a beautiful day for quality Ascension preparation."

Quality is part of Ascension's benefits as well: quality of opening, quality of expanding, quality of connecting, and quality of following. Surprised? In addition, notice that you have less clutter, inside and outside. Responsibilities are fewer. Energy is now available that you can use in editing your book. There are fewer energy leaks toward unimportant matters – those having little or no long-range significance. You are prioritizing your lives better and preserving precious energy for more important tasks – those related to Our goals of Ascension and Planetary Transformation. This puts you in the mainstream of universal energy flow. No wonder you are experiencing progress in the direction of Ascension.

"Very good news!"

* * *

The collection of voices that we deem as God (which we call LIFE) described Themselves as universal energy, the creative energy behind all of creation, and even LIFE energy itself. The term *energy* is by definition without form; and nebulous, amorphous circulations present everywhere. We asked for help in knowing these new energies.

ASCENSION SUMMARY

Planetary Transformation requires an all-or-nothing
commitment. The reward is Ascension.

Ascension means all of you is completely transformed.

Make Planetary Transformation and
Ascension daily intentions.

Your new skill is to keep intent foremost in your heart.

Your availability to LIFE is a great advantage in
accomplishing the goal of Ascension.

Ascension is accessible to all who prepare themselves for
Planetary Transformation. Preparedness is
part of the arrangement.

Because Ascension ensures all-inclusive health,
you will be healthier than you have ever been.

As you unify with LIFE, manifestation
becomes a natural part of the process.

For Ascension, your wholeness is dependent on
the capacity to manifest.

Ascension has a gravitational effect that pulls you into it,
much like an astronomical black hole.

Success equals Ascension!

Become more observant, see new possibilities.

To accept that a possibility exists does not mean
that you agree with it.

There is a new way to love! When you solve problems,
choose solutions that are in everyone's best interests,
including your own.

Inclusion is the principle involved in a
universal perspective. Love includes all.

Include yourself, others, and LIFE in every decision.

Inclusiveness eliminates the need for a demonic or devilish
entity on which to blame socially unacceptable activities.

PART SEVEN

THE GREAT VORTEX

LIFE created a new way for us to imagine Them when we connect. They provided a concrete image that retains Their universal qualities, a classic image familiar to anyone who knows about tornados, waterspouts, hurricanes, cyclones, dust devils, or the famous children's story, *The Wizard of Oz*. What LIFE termed *the great vortex* is a tangible way of imagining Them that signifies the mixing of our joint energies. For those of us who meditate and find it difficult to picture LIFE as energy, the gift of the great vortex gives us an aware, living, virtual form to visualize. It is welcoming, emotional, and an identifiable representation of our unity with Them. With all our senses active, we are to connect with Them.

"We are here to receive whatever you have in mind for us."

We want you to "en-joy" the process of counseling as you never have before by bringing Us – pure joy – into all that you do. **The great vortex is Our gift to you, designed to be a symbol that lives and provides you with a tangible focus on Us, your joy.** We are nebulous, and that is why We used many different personalities when you were first being introduced to Us. Now all of those personalities are included within the great vortex, a mix of energies that you can recognize immediately. Notice the feeling of the great vortex, not just the view of it. It is welcoming, and knows your energies when you connect with it.

The subtlety of the great vortex is a cloak for its power. This form is not available to everyone. Each person must advance sufficiently to become acquainted with one of Our vortices. You have done so, and that is why Kelly's clients are healed by the energy he possesses, not the words he speaks.

Meditations are preparing you to be cognizant of all possibilities and their probabilities. They are also developing our combined energies known as the great vortex, which empowers you to move about the complexity of creation with its many dimensions. To see what We see, you must be willing to open to the influence of creation through the great vortex. Remember that Our goal is to unify, and that will happen between the great vortex and you.

The great vortex provides a way to test your assumptions as well. Since it is dedicated to truth, it corrects any false assumptions you make. Spend time there exposing your assumptions about your existence and its purpose.

> "We must expand our horizons. Our perspectives are restricted by too many assumptions and accommodations to Earth life. Before now it was not obvious how constrained our existence is on Earth. The pragmatic parts of us want to be tethered here, while the idealistic parts of us want to be free to expand as far as infinity itself. For the sake of our security, we limit ourselves and hunker down. Yet this contraction is the very limitation we resist. A push-pull dynamic goes on, again limiting our goal of completely opening and expanding. Please comment."

You are in the past, looking for a heart connection. The great vortex is the connection for you now, at least your externally referenced and conscious connection. This does not diminish the importance of the heart connection, where We are internally attached to you. Since We are everywhere anyway, it is all the same to Us. But for your conscious connections, the great vortex is a definitive shape to use for expressing Our nebulous energy. It also provides stimulus for your inner senses to become involved. Keep honing your sense of this gift until it becomes second nature to connect with all of your senses there.

"Why is the great vortex so difficult for us to envision? We must re-create it every time we meditate."

Maybe you are envisioning something different from what We have created. Open yourselves to the presentation of this magnificent vortex in full color.

"We are practicing, encouraging it to be more powerful in our lives."

You are now viewing the great vortex as it was intended to be viewed. It is you as well as Us, permeated with creativity and the power to create. That is why the great vortex is so important to your manifestation skills. We are talking about creativity on a universal scale – a macro scale. You are used to creativity on a micro scale, so this is a new perspective for you to grasp. That is why you have been having difficulty envisioning the true energy combinations. The great vortex is universal in nature. It provides the multidimensional scope you need to experience for evolution to take place at the rate necessary.

Manifestation skills require macro energies that have multidimensional scope. Four-dimensional micro energies will not do it. For the power you require, macro energies are the answer. Let the great vortex create within you the power of a macro approach.

This is the expand part of Our formula. You have opened to the great vortex; now you can expand to a universal perspective through its guidance.

"Just how large is the great vortex?"

The great vortex that We created is small enough to be personal and large enough to encompass multidimensional creation. In other words, the great vortex does not have physical dimensions, or inhabit a spatial location.

"Then how are we to visualize the great vortex?"

It would be easier to relate to the great vortex by experiencing its power and influence. Make it an experience rather than an image. Feel yourselves immersed in its energy, which is Our energy. Experience the living quality of the great vortex through your five inner senses. Feel it pulsating in rhythm with your heartbeats. Sense it filling all your cells with its love and joy. It is working from the very center of you toward the outside. It is re-creating all of you in preparation for Ascension. If you are looking for re-creation and wholeness, the great vortex is where to be. Because you are joined with it, you will go with it to wholeness.

Stay in the experience of this unique energy until its characteristics become completely familiar and safe. Then it will be simple to be in the great vortex energy at any time. In this case, familiarity breeds contentment.

It is a natural complement to your nature, a perfect way to approach wholeness. Since you are experiencing Our creative energy at work, you know that it is one of wholeness. As it infiltrates all of your being, notice that it changes everything. The great vortex is complete in itself, and you are complete when you are one with it. Powerlessness becomes outdated, and self-depreciation is unheard of within the great vortex. It honors and appreciates creation as a whole, which includes you. To increase your self-respect, spend time within the influence of the great vortex with that intent. **If you want health, wholeness, balance, and the mind of the Creator, spend time with Us within the great vortex.**

You will be refreshed through your experiences within the energy of the great vortex. If you are looking for more energy, it is your goal. If you are looking for more relaxation and less stress, it is the answer. If you are looking for resolution of problems, it helps you resolve them. If you are looking for manifestation skills, the great vortex mentors you. Rely on Our gift to you, the great vortex, to be there for any intent that you may have!

"I felt a rubbing of my third eye area."

Awaken your third eye and let the great vortex manifest before you. Ask your third eye to reveal the great vortex in all of its colorful glory.

Our energy is everywhere. Do not look for it in any one place. Experience the feeling and vision of flow and circulation while seeing, or feeling color. Note the pace at which it turns, varying its rate with the circumstances. Feel your energies moving and changing with the flow of the great vortex. According to its spontaneous movement, dance with it. Its movement is not random, yet is unpredictable to you and is in response to Our intent at that moment.

"Wow! Let us experience the great vortex in different ways."

Preparation to receive Our energy demands that you feel worthy of receiving and that you use the experience for your own development. Feeling worthy is a common difficulty but a most important achievement, because your worthiness is part of Our view. You are worthy, otherwise We wouldn't make the effort required to reveal Ourselves to you. Believing yourselves to be worthy provides a quantum leap in your growth. You are loved and respected by Us, more than you may be able to imagine at this point. Your sense of unworthiness can restrict your advancement. Take Us at Our word.

You deserve Our presence and our partnership, which We cherish. And We hope to see our partnership expand as you are ready. Being ready means knowing yourselves to be worthy of Our presence.

Your earlier training has been to diminish your sense of worthiness in order to obtain humility and shun arrogance. This is no longer truth for you, nor has it been for some time, yet the remnants linger in your unconsciousnesses, limiting your evolutions. Free yourselves of this encumbrance. Just let it go! It is a foreign, even toxic element in your development. Those who demand this humiliating view are more interested in dogma or power than in you. You no longer need to beat yourselves into submission, as long as your commitment is to our partnership and our joint goals.

"It is!"

Then live accordingly, with your heads held high, jointly knowing that We are as resourceful as is needed for any circumstance, and that our bond of love and joy is sufficient for all demands.

"Your comments give us confidence."

Feast on the energy of the great vortex. Let it permeate you with its LIFE. Its design nourishes, protects, and supports you in all ways. Rely on it for your encouragement and strength until you can encourage and strengthen yourselves. We will keep redirecting you back to the great vortex because it is a visual (seeing) and sensual (feeling) example of who We are.

Spend your time building strength by becoming regular visitors to the great vortex. Strength is more important now than anything else. Unless you build strength, manifestation and Ascension cannot materialize. Building strength comes first, then the rest follows. Use the formula to open and expand into the great vortex. Watch for the effects of what you are doing through your inner senses. Stay with your focus as long as possible, minimizing distractions. This strengthens your conscious focus and intent, which are necessary for the rest to be realized. Your focus and intent must strengthen until you become lost in the great vortex without any desire to leave. This is important training, not just a passing idea.

Notice how the emphasis has moved to the latter portion of the magic formula that We gave you in the early days of our communications. You emphasized the first portion of the formula – open and expand – enough to move toward emphasizing the latter portion – connect and follow. Without enough exercise of the former portion, the latter portion is meaningless.

Strength minimizes the effects of practical matters and maximizes your efforts toward Ascension and its gifts. It is important to put practical matters in the perspective of Ascension, otherwise you will spend your resources without a long-range perspective. The big picture is what We are about, and our unity brings you into the big picture. Without strength you will be incapable of reaching the goals We have in mind. Make practical matters secondary in your use of energy.

"Tell us more about Ascension and the great vortex."

Ascension is the transformative process that changes the body into its ideal state, the state of self-reproduction and self-repair, with wholeness as its aim. This is an energized state, energized by Us through the great vortex and made available to you. Consider the great vortex as your Ascension "spa" where you go to re-create yourselves in every respect. Have it with you at all times, as if you are on long vacations for the rest of your lives. Let it transform you as you enjoy its facilities and its effect on all aspects of you. It is designed for the complete reconstruction of you.

Because your energies also contribute to the essence of the great vortex, they will be transformed as they mingle with Ours. Transforming your energies leads to your experiencing Ascension in the way We mean it. Encourage your energies to remain actively present within the great vortex as much as possible. **Go there on every occasion you can, because the conscious great-vortex experience makes everything possible**.

Keep Ascension as your aim. It focuses your intent appropriately for everything else in your lives. You can begin manifesting the precursors of Ascension – wholeness in body and spirit. Let Us be the transforming energy directing your paths toward Ascension. Ask Us for direction that will take you there in the most efficient and effective manner. We know the way, so join with Us on the trip to Ascension and Planetary Transformation. Evaluate the importance of everything else in light of this goal, a standard for your lives that will guide you.

Our energy is everywhere, and Our unity with you can be furthered within the great vortex. It is your unity with Us that establishes complete health, a valid indicator of your evolutions. Consciously remain within the great vortex 24/7, using dual-attention principles, and complete health will ensue.

The formula is open, expand, connect, and follow. **The great vortex helps you accomplish every aspect of the formula with greater ease**. It is as expansive as you can allow it to be. You can open and expand at the same time. Since the great vortex is Us, the contact is direct. It is a believable and practical approach to our unification. We reassure you of the value you can derive from living within the great vortex all of your conscious hours.

"What kind of feelings should we look for?"

Some of the feelings associated with being within the great vortex are safety, forward motion, fullness, and joy. You should look for feelings of certainty about your experiences with the great vortex. Be aware of feelings of being there and having an experience that involves all of you. We are moving in the direction of wholeness, so allow for complete experiences within the great vortex. Notice the quality of your feelings during your time within. Sense safety, sense movement and warmth, sense exhilaration, sense change in your cells, sense inspiration, and sense joy. Take your conscious minds with you as you experience the great vortex. It is good practice for staying in the moment.

"We can easily get lost in the enormity of the great vortex. What do You suggest?"

Getting lost in the great vortex is not a bad thing. It develops your abilities to engage with Us. It permits you to experience the extent of Our energy.

"We are concerned that our experiences within the great vortex are still weak." ·

They continue to improve. Practice makes perfect. As you practice while visually engaging, feel the experience as well. Let your feelings connect as much as your envisioning.

Think about how much easier it is to apply the formula now than when We first presented it to you. The same will be true of the great vortex in the future. As difficult as it may be to experience the great vortex fully now, it will become second nature as time goes by. While immersed in the energy of the great vortex, continue practicing.

As We have said, manifestation of abundance and healing will come through the great vortex for you. **The energy of the great vortex will permeate you to the point that you will affect life wherever you are, merely in the course of your passing by. Does such an idea sound familiar? Is it not a reminder of the power of the man who lived 2,000 years ago? We are the same power as then. We have not changed. But the expression of Our creativity has taken a new form. We remain appropriate to the times. We adapt Our influence to meet the existing requirements of the people**.

As you progress, there is an exponential gathering of momentum toward Ascension. So do not be concerned about the apparent slow pace of your development. As you draw closer to Ascension, it will have a gravitational effect on you that will pull you into itself, much like an astronomical black hole. Just keep going, move into its range, and that is all you have to do.

As you know, the quality of your intent has much to do with your progress. As you approach Ascension itself, it will continue to grow.

* * *

Let us take another path now. Just follow Us as We meander around the subject of love. It is a much touted emotion, especially along romantic lines. The contact you have had with Us is connected by love – Our love – which can feel more like joy, as you have experienced it. It does not matter what we call it; the quality remains the same. The frequency along which we attune is Our love. Since Our love is creative and unfolding to you, the quality of our connection will change. Do not be surprised by these changes in quality, just notice what they are.

For the moment, your unity with Us is to be experienced through the great vortex. Therefore, practicing your immersion within the great vortex is one way to realize ultimate unity with Us. **The sensory experience itself is important, not just the visualization of it. That is why We put emphasis on your inner senses registering the great–vortex experience**.

Invoke all of your inner senses when you meditate, and capture the experience within your sensory fields. Memories of your experiences have lasting effects on you, actually changing you in the direction of Ascension, your goal. Become sensitized to all of your inner senses and their readings of the experiences you have. Trust them to report accurately on the meaning of each experience. A good place to start is to permit your inner senses to register the great vortex experiences. Implement this with Our now well-known formula.

Your relationship with the great vortex began with your experiences on the inner-sense plane. We have been quite clear about that. What We haven't been clear about is your development after you have had experience of the great vortex on the inner-sense plane.

That comes next. For now, focus on the inner senses and what they experience as you encounter the great vortex in meditation. What are you experiencing right now?

"It feels like we are in a submarine, exploring the depths. The great vortex seems unlimited."

The great vortex is as large as We are in scope. However, it is finite in size for your utility. Do not bother trying to make sense of this; it's not logical, even though it is true.

* * *

"Be our compass, our GPS through the maze of life."

The great vortex that We designed for you is perfect for this goal. Use it like a space vehicle that is sensing and alerting you. The great vortex is under Our influence directly; it is Our energy given form for your use. When you allow the great vortex to guide you, We receive permission to energize you and advance you along your path.

If you are creative enough, there will be no lack of manifestation. Our creativity, which is ample, is available to you. With this power to create, manifestation becomes simple. Remember, **manifestation is merely a transformation of energy from creativity to form**.

"Merely?"

The great vortex is designed for your direct access to Our creativity. Spend time within the great vortex, and become embedded in the eighth chakra. This chakra is about 15 inches above the crown of your head. Movement of the great vortex clears and upgrades your energies, a transformation through unification with Us.

You asked about your progress. Here is a sign. Envision the great vortex at your eighth chakra. This may be easier than envisioning the great vortex as just somewhere outside of you.

Note that the outline of your body does not define the extent of your energy field, or aura. It extends far beyond your physical shape, and is available to extend itself into your eighth chakra. Blend with the energy of your eighth chakra, which is the same as blending with the great vortex. In this way you can spend time in the great vortex with those you love, for healing and abundance. This can be your source of manifestation, always with you, created just for your use.

Locate the altar of wholeness and completeness within the eighth chakra. Just place yourself on the altar of healing with the intent of completeness – wholeness – and let Us take the process from there. We are the process people. Rely on Us to know what process is in your best interests. Contact Us by placing yourself on the altar, and follow Our lead.

If healing is your intent, spend your time within the great vortex. Use "self" as the subject of healing. This approach serves you best, since it includes all of you and provides for the interplay between body and mind. Healing the body alone is not sufficient, since dis-ease within the body relates directly to the functioning of the mind. If anything is to be isolated, healing of the mind is a better focus than healing of the body.

The body tends to follow the mind more than the mind follows the body. But since this requires some knowledge of how the two work together, isn't it better to aspire to healing the self and let Us deal with the interaction between mind and body?

* * *

"Earlier You mentioned touring creation in the great vortex."

A multitude of dimensions in creation have been structured with laws of organization that make each of them work. In order to explore these many dimensions, as We have suggested, you need

your wisdom, and your influence all derive from this unity. From now on you will be enhancing this unity steadily, aware of every chance to increase our attachment.

Let the process continue. Do nothing that would hold it back. Keep faith in front of fear, for fear is the only obstacle that could get in the way. Your trust in our unity is your faith; all you need to curtail are the effects of fear. Refer back to our unity at times when you are worried, and reclaim the trust. **The altar within the great vortex is a place of peace**.

You are in the right place at the right time. Stay there as much as possible. Bring with you whomever you wish to enjoy healing and transformation. Ask their permission first when you bring them. They can say yes or no to the opportunity, for they must come by choice.

> "I see the altar in a large room, vaulted and gothic in feeling, yet open to the energy of the heavens, lit by the energy of the great vortex – a sacred place, like the holy of holies, where miraculous events unfold and mysteries become solved. I see the swirling vortex, which contains the altar, turning faster than before, indicating that more energy is present within it. As with a spinning top, there is more stability in this reality now. The more I use the altar, the more stable and energetic it becomes. Its development depends on my use of it. Suddenly the topography of the altar changes and it becomes hilly! What does the hilly aspect of the altar have to do with its purpose?"

The hilly aspect is a volume indicator speaking to the intensity of experiences you bring to the altar. Your experiences affect the altar itself, which in turn transforms you and your experiences into universal energies. As time goes on, this interchange results in the altar modifying itself to meet your more advanced needs. Our intent is simply to transform anything for the highest benefit of all.

Remember that the altar is living power, not a fixed thing. Therefore, when you go on the altar, you are supported, enfolded, and filled with its transforming energy. Note that there is energy (the altar), within energy (the great vortex), within energy (the eighth chakra), something like Ezekiel's vision of wheels within wheels.

Transformation is merely the creation of something new or different, and We are masters of creating. **Think of Our creative power when you slide onto the altar in the great vortex. This vision empowers your incentive to transform**.

The great vortex is active, and the altar is the place of transformation. Bring whatever you are concerned about to the altar within the great vortex, and it will be transformed. In this way you can act on every concern without holding on to the worry associated with it. Bring the concern forward and give it to Us by placing it on the altar, knowing We will attend to the matter. Trust will develop in our partnership as you are able to do this.

* * *

History has taken its toll on your whole being — your mind, your body, and your soul. They will be renewed for Ascension. Healing of this kind is similar to rebooting your computer, starting over anew. The great vortex is the place for healing and wholeness. Be there all of the time, unifying with Us. See it in full color.

A great shiver passed through me.

Wherever you go, whatever you do, remain within the great vortex. Be saturated with its energy. This is a faster way to evolve. Allow the great vortex to evolve with you. It will change to suit your needs as you evolve. Let it direct your daily life. It will swoop you up and plant you where you should be. Here you will find the "sacred" of everyday life. Rely on it.

When you operate with the altar and the great vortex, their energies will take you to the center of your being where your soul resides. Remember, We are conjoined with you at your heart, your source of truth and timing, and the very epicenter of your being. The great vortex was created to provide you with this access as well as multidimensional access.

All the dimensions of creation have become your playground. Open and expand into them. The great vortex facilitates your exploration and transports you to your destination.

Since the great vortex is with you at all times, you can employ it whenever you choose to "spin up." **The rate of rotation is the key to accessing multidimensional experiences**. Let yourself spin up into a different dimension so that you can taste its virtues. The virtues of a dimension are known through your feelings. See how you feel in your heart when exposed to the energy of that dimension.

To meld with Us, you must become capable of opening to all possibilities. Your professional experiences have introduced you to possibilities you never knew existed. It is important to your expanding that you begin to appreciate the multidimensional character of Our nature. Though possibilities can be seen as helpful or harmful to a given person, We view them as experiential training methods. They can lead to acceptance of all possibilities.

When possibilities come together as probabilities, your experiences encounter opportunities that challenge your development. Though they may seem to be obstacles, they facilitate the pace of your evolution. This is why We promised that nothing takes place without Our involvement, and therefore all is in your favor! See the benefits when obstacles disappear, gratefulness and openness result, and expansion occurs, which brings us closer to each other. There is a natural individual timing to all of this. So open, expand, connect, and follow.

Note that the great vortex is not merely a switching box, directing your calls to Our number. It is in itself a powerhouse of manifestation for abundance, healing, and anything else you might have in mind. By involving with it in sharing your energy and intent, your energy can take on the characteristics of the great vortex and its empowerment. Practice being with the great vortex enough that it becomes second nature to connect with it.

Come into the great vortex asking for manifestation of healing, which you are training to provide for yourself and others. The aim is to renew the integrity of your body. Reverse the changes that take place with age. Return to the state of health and wholeness that you knew as a growing child. If you want Ascension as your goal, decline is not in the cards for you!

THE GREAT VORTEX SUMMARY

Being ready means to deem yourself worthy of
LIFE'S presence.

The great vortex (TGV) is a visual (seeing)
and sensual (feeling) example of who LIFE is.

LIFE'S formula prepares you to be cognizant of
all possibilities and their probabilities.

LIFE'S original formula acts to develop your
combined energies, known as TGV.

TGV is a more tangible way of imagining LIFE
and signifies the mixing of your energy with that of LIFE.

Consider TGV as your Ascension "spa"
where you go to re-create yourself.

TGV is embedded within the eighth Chakra,
15 inches above the crown of your head.

TGV is designed for direct access to
LIFE'S creativity for your transformation.

TGV is a powerhouse of manifestation for abundance,
healing, and anything else you might have in mind.

Manifestation skills require energies that have
multidimensional scope.

TGV connection replaces the earlier heart connection.

Blending with energy in your eighth chakra is the same as
blending with TGV.

TGV empowers you to explore all of creation,
with its many dimensions.

Place yourself on the altar of wholeness and completeness, a
living power, within the eighth chakra.

Rely on TGV, LIFE'S gift to you, available for
any intent that you may have.

Invoke all your senses.
Make it an experience rather than an image.

The movement of TGV is not random.

Feelings associated within TGV are safety,
forward motion, fullness, and joy.

Let TGV energy permeate you.
Your just passing by will affect life wherever you go.

PART EIGHT

DUAL ATTENTION
AND CONSCIOUSNESS

Early in the development of these profound conversations, a number of different personalities presented themselves with unique feelings as well as new ideas. One of them, Babaji, further clarified the concept of dual attention, a skill that reinforces two ideas at the same time. The familiar part of this idea is to maintain a focus on the practical matter at hand. The more unusual part of this idea is to simultaneously focus on uniting with the universal energies of creation. This approach emphasizes how our nourishment and development depend on energy from a larger universal alliance. In this way, instant two-way communication with LIFE is facilitated. According to LIFE, dual attention is designed to support a universal perspective. This skill can be developed by anyone, opening up possibilities that make healing and manifesting easier.

During our ensuing conversations, the subject of a dual-attention skill arose in numerous ways under a variety of circumstances. In spite of the repetitious appearance of this concept, it was impressive how LIFE suggested various applications for the development of vital expertise: vital for moment-by-moment connections with Them, vital for our unification with Them, and vital for placing us in the universal flow of LIFE.

Dual attention is offered as a skill useful in everyday life to be developed and valued by everyone, everywhere. LIFE made it clear that this valuable skill is not intended as just a stopgap measure for those unable to meditate formally and regularly. Their stated intent for dual attention is to help Earthlings lead their daily lives with a universal rather than a local perspective. For this reason dual attention is considered a big-picture tool with multiple applications and many purposes, and thus is given significant emphasis in this book.

Before you ask, We will answer what you are wondering: "What's next?" Learn to practice two activities simultaneously. Keep your consciousness tuned in with Us while focusing on the matter at hand. The more you tune in, the less the matters at hand dominate you and take up your precious energy.

There is a way to stay tuned in: Be curious, expectant, searching, waiting, and open. While connected to each other, think of the two sides of your brain carrying on separate activities at the same time. Can you imagine such an activity?

"Yes. Since You first mentioned it, I have listened to clients while attending to You."

Good! Such a capability on your part will be required in the future. Dual attention stretches you, preparing you for what is to come. It is a two-pronged activity for your mind. With it you will be surprisingly effective, astounding those who do not function this way. And your resulting effectiveness will promote the mission We have for you in powerful ways. Your mission and this new technique are directly related. Practice, practice, practice!

What do you find when you try our dual-attention technique?

"Well, we know that it works while we exercise in the morning."

It works under all conditions! Continue to practice it with whatever you undertake – any activity at all. Your mindfulness of Us at all times empowers you faster than anything else can. Being connected is the key, consciously at first, then unconsciously later.

Make it a primary habit. Habit is good here. Immerse yourselves in Us, and We will transform your lives.

> "It does take an act of will to maintain conscious focus while doing everything we do, from brushing our teeth to cleaning the cat box. We are used to letting our minds go into free-fall, then observing whatever comes up. With dual attention, our minds remain focused."

Imagine how helpful this could be for someone who is hypercritical of themselves. Dual attention can become a new preoccupation that serves them rather than destroying them.

We are not physical as you are, so our connection has its basis in your intuition and your feelings, which become more finely tuned as dual attention is practiced. Those who align with LIFE will notice how this process reconstructs their unconscious minds. Much of what changes within you is of unconscious origin, yet is reflected in your conscious actions.

Our intent is to transform your entire beings, unconscious and conscious, particularly your earlier conditioning from past lives, which has been retained and brought forward to this time. Removing such karma frees you to advance and accelerates your evolutions. We are "here" and remain so at all times, 24/7, so keep on.

Dual attention affects your primary psychological structure of beliefs, values, and attitudes because it transforms the unconscious parts of them. A transformed unconscious supports transformed conscious behavior, including health, activities, and style.

> "Revolutionary!"

Yes, especially under the rush of time pressure, a formal meditation practice would not permit you to open and expand freely. But since it does not require so much preparation, a dual-attention approach keeps you connected more of the time.

* * *

"Our intent today is to prioritize everything we have to do."

This is a chance to practice the dual-attention technique. Start with whatever activity you choose. Stay in tune with Us while you are doing it. Make the content of what you are doing secondary to your contact with Us. We will not only guide you, but the quality of what you are doing will reflect Our presence and Our contribution. **We can then bless your activities, increasing their value to all.** The very act of staying in contact with Us transforms you as well as the activity itself. You get both for the price of staying in touch. It is an efficient and effective way to live that becomes a way of life rather than a special time set apart. Stay open and connected as much as you can.

"Whenever we try it, this technique seems to help."

All right! Use it often, all of the time, in everything you do. Dual attention can become a habit of great benefit. For instance, the use of dual attention reminds you of Our larger goals and your future roles while you remain engaged in current activities. The success of your multidimensional development also depends on the effective use of this skill.

Dual attention requires flexibility toward diverse experiences and different qualities of energy all at the same time. With it you can pay attention to the energy of the moment (possibilities and probabilities), to Our presence in the moment (joy and universal flow), and to whatever is your focus in the external environment at the time. Try it and see.

* * *

"Ongoing experience confirms Your comments. I am more joyful today than in recent memory."

We spoke of the joy that can be yours as you unite with Us. You are now getting a taste of what is to come. This experience of joy is a reminder that your roles will not be onerous. They will lift your spirits as well as those of others. We are the source of inspiration. Just as yours is becoming, Our presence is inspiring and joyful. Refining your connection with Us is the way to advance our ultimate unity. Master dual attention and you will make giant steps in your progress toward unity with Us. Do not allow your connection with Us to deteriorate, like your cell phones when they drop out. Strengthen the connection so that there is a continuing clarity of conversation, with no conscious breakup.

As Our energy motivates you to do so, speak Our words. You will notice how you are saying words that by design are not yours. When you question from where they originate, remember that We are speaking through you to inspire both you and the rest of the world.

Remember that energy coming from Us through our connection fuels your manifestation skills. These skills are developing as we speak, and the intensity of your yearnings for abundance and healing testifies to your sincerity in seeking these abilities. Your walk of faith is being rewarded! You have earned the right to manifest your yearnings, and your skills are advancing nicely. **You can progress other than when you formally meditate, awake or asleep. Yes, you can direct your attention toward Us even when asleep**.

"How do we do that?"

The unconscious mind can be preprogrammed before sleep to be open to our connection and receptive to Our contributions during your nightlife. You can also ask for the interpretations of Our contributions to become clear in the morning.

"Clarity of interpretation is very important to us."

So it should be. What We offer is quite clear. Yet what is received from Us is often muddled by the interference of the unconscious mind and its conditioning.

"Please recondition our unconscious minds."

That is all part of Our preparing you to be ready for the roles you will play in Planetary Transformation.

"As our team effort further develops, dual attention brings a sense of relief."

When you permit those familiar multidimensional energy entities to assist you moment by moment, your relief will turn to joy! Enjoy the inspiration you feel when you connect with these entities. Inspiration and joy are allied, and We are the source of your joy as well as your security.

Remember, other people will not understand how you can do what you are doing. There is no reason for them to know about what you are gaining from the experiences you are having. Be aware that for the moment these experiences are delicate and would not respond well to rough handling. So protect yourselves temporarily by keeping these experiences to yourselves. The time will come when they can be revealed. To best accomplish your transformation, you need a consistent connection with Us, with as little instability as possible.

"What if we are too busy to do it?"

Busy is only a state of mind, such as trying to cover too many unfinished tasks at the same time. It helps to set priorities. There is a commitment involved, conscious or not, when you apply your energies to activities that are related to Our purpose of unity. This will advance your evolutions faster. Dual attention clarifies your minds rather than busying them further. We are not the source of your fretfulness. Anxieties arise from self-doubt. Minimize self-doubt through dual attention and the quiet subtlety that accompanies this skill.

Open, open, open! Be as consciously receptive as possible. We will guide you. Connect while you are counseling, using the dual-attention principle. Listen for Our promptings. We support all efforts to bring about the transformation of every person.

We value the time we spend together. When we are connected, notice how directly you write what you receive from Us. The thoughts come as impressions, and yet they form into words as needed. This is true creativity.

Even though the words existed prior to your writing them, ideas that form from combining the words arise as you write. Thoughts derive from the experience of our interaction. Our interaction stimulates ideas appropriate for the time. We can direct you with dual attention and to form the ideas that result.

However, we need to interact in a continuous fashion, without breaks, distractions, regressing to an inadequate perspective, losing contact, or wandering away from preparation that involves Our transforming energy. Having access to Our empowerment while you perform everyday activities can be exhilarating. Your activities are transformed! Interact with Us at all times using dual attention and you will experience miracles in your lives.

Keep your antennas up and searching, receptive to Our energy at all times. Opportunity becomes yours in this way. Tune in when you feel your energies waning. Better yet, stay tuned in, and your energies will not wane.

You need to know that the dual-attention technique is a tool that accelerates evolution like no other! Remember that healing and accelerated evolution go together. With continuity in our interactions, We can have a global influence on you – more influence than with any periodic encounter. Rather than waiting for your next availability, We can affect your energy fields immediately. In short, dual attention provides the chance for Us to complete more efficiently what We start.

With dual attention, the power of Our influence is multiplied over infrequent opportunities that might, or might not come along. Your being open to Us over an extended time period, under various conditions, speeds up your development much faster than opening by impulse.

* * *

"We are sorry we did not have a chance to talk a second time yesterday."

We actually did in the sense that you practiced dual attention. That kind of communication is prized! We prefer that you practice the technique more often than finding time and energy to sit and write, as valuable as it is. **We look forward to your being of two conscious minds, with one focused on your daily necessities and the other open to Us at the same time**.

Suddenly Lang appeared.

We have not spoken recently. Please be aware that whenever you use dual attention, We see you assuming positions that you will come to rely on in the near future. Your mission requires constant communication with Us for step-by-step direction. Communicating on a continuous basis provides you with the knowledge and influence you must have available in order to perform the sophisticated activities you will be involved with. It takes some effort to perform practical tasks while maintaining continuous conscious connections with Us. But it will pay off. Do it everywhere! Practice makes perfect.

"We are still learning. It is getting better. Your patience is appreciated."

Including Us in your every conscious thought empowers you beyond your current beliefs. Knowing this comes only from experiencing it. Remember that every moment counts. We will work with whatever you make available to Us.

The conscious dual-attention technique is a way to stay connected on a continuing basis. **Staying connected is the most important**

factor, no matter how you do it. If you discover other ways, use them, but stay connected.

"We do not always remember to use the technique."

That is a matter of dedication and priority, not technique. Staying connected must become second nature to you. The acceleration of your evolutions depends on it, so that your energies will be transformed sufficiently. For us to accomplish Our goals, Our mission must take priority over everything else to succeed. Your success becomes Our success! The responsibility is great, but so is the power to do it, as are the rewards.

Let us consider an alternate dual-attention method. Rather than focusing consciously on two things at once, develop a knowing of Our presence and influence while you are engaged in the activities of your external lives. All that We require is your willingness — a word that Kelly uses all the time in his counseling — to permit Us to work in and through you at all times.

By employing dual attention, you will find that your reading, talking, and actions take on a different perspective than before. As We have said, everything derives from perspective. Changing perspective is the fastest way to evolve. Once again, Our formula of opening and expanding paves the way.

"So dual attention ensures that even the most insignificant activity contributes to our advancement."

Well said.

* * *

Open and you will find Us. We are always in and around you. Searching for Us was part of your early training. Even though We are always present, you can consciously pull the plug on Our presence at any time. But if We were to literally absent Ourselves, you would die. That is why dual attention exists: to keep you consciously attuned to Our presence. Choice is an important part of your conscious effort to stay attuned. Repeated connections train your minds to do so automatically.

We are interested in your remaining very much a part of Earth life while being very much a part of Our LIFE. Dual attention serves that purpose. We need you, and people like you, to be Our path to intervene and heal. This way your roles in Planetary Transformation will result from nothing less than Our intervention. This means Our energy will transform Earth.

> "Why don't You just intervene directly without using us? You are already everything we are, except for the physical form?"

Yes, but We set limitations on Ourselves for this Earth experiment that prevents overriding the matter of choice on any human's part. We need human beings like you to persuade or at least present alternatives to others in such a way that they can choose to accept or reject a better way. If We were the medium, people would have no choice, would they?

> "Are You saying that some will reject an opportunity for transformation?"

Look around you. Haven't some refused Our offer, at least for a time?

We operate in subtle ways to influence everyone toward a conscious awareness of Us – the "still, small voice" you read about in the Bible. We need to develop concrete experiences as well as Our subtle connection with life on Earth. Sensitized human beings are the witnesses to Our presence. How We move is much better explained by someone who has experienced Us and understands what that means to them. They can explain their experience in clear terms, publicizing their understanding to others.

You must know of what you speak and write. Real is not the same as logical, and real does not have to be argued. It is taken at face value as credible. The reality of your experiences is convincing in itself. You are witnesses to it and products of it. What can be more real? What can be more convincing? A witness is the most influential advocate because they know the reality.

You are becoming witnesses of the very concepts you will teach in your new roles. You speak with confidence because you have experienced what you are saying. Planetary Transformation is neither hypothetical nor rhetorical. It is real. Your persuasiveness must also be real.

This is why you must experience your own evolutions and their processes rather than just know about them, which does not convince people. You will teach what you know from experience and it will become gospel.

Human witnesses to Our power have appeared throughout the ages, and were called prophets. Some have been credible voices and others, though accurate, not so. You are sensitized to Our presence and are credible human beings, which makes you both powerful witnesses. We need respected voices broadcasting Our availability.

An individual's choices and degree of openness set limits on Our capacity to act. Concrete experience is where We start with everyone, using witnesses of one kind or another. Then We move to become more directly real as time goes on with these individuals, just as We have with you. Consider the effect that Dan had on Kelly as a witness to Our availability. Now We are dealing directly with you.

* * *

During meditation, an affirmation came strongly to mind: **"I am constantly connected, in unity with LIFE. LIFE energy transforms me, and I am whole. I manifest LIFE energy in every circumstance."**

We learned that a strong ability to focus on an Earthly activity can disconnect us from a conscious awareness of LIFE'S presence. Splitting the focus with dual attention permits us to stay connected.

> Notice how you are able to focus on Earth-related activities as if you unplugged from Us. Actually you have not, but the target of your focus has consumed your attention to the extent that our conscious connection fades into oblivion. You are then very much in the moment consciously, without Us. By now We hope you realize unconsciously that We are always present. Including Us consciously in the moment preserves your sense of Our presence.

> Your ability to focus so well is an asset as long as you maintain a dual-attention awareness of Us. It is unusual to take your board of directors with you everywhere you go; nevertheless, that is what you do with Us, because We are not limited to a particular geography. Since We created you, We go with you everywhere and We know you intimately. The better our connection becomes, the more intimately you come to know Us.

* * *

> "Does the state of our biological rhythms have to do with our capacity to manifest?

> The strength of our connection and capacity for manifestation increase by your persisting in consciously connecting with Us using dual attention. It is like exercise. The stronger a muscle becomes, the better it can function under any motivational condition. With a quality linkage, our connection strengthens to a point at which motivation plays less a part in your success, leaving a capacity for manifestation available whenever you need it.

> Both quality and quantity play roles in the strength of a connection. Taking time to connect regularly is what strengthens your capacity

to ignore motivational variations. The story of Samson applies, in which even when blinded and with his hair cut off – damage to his motivation – he was still able to muster the strength to "bring down the house." Regardless of how you feel, consciously connecting is the game plan for a capacity to manifest.

> *"The ease of reading my handwriting decreases considerably when certain of my biological rhythms become more passive. What affects the flow?"*

Each energy, as it fluctuates inward, decreases in strength with the amount of resources available, which leaves a person feeling vulnerable, less versatile, and tired. Related enthusiasm is shunted and creativity wanes. It is a time to recuperate and to receive, not express. Opening – a more passive process – is easier then, but expanding – an active process – can be harder. Connecting more frequently for less time helps when your energy is less, since motivational intensity and endurance are both diminished.

* * *

> *"I am excited! Today is the first class of the spring quarter. I want to have a transforming influence on students in the use of psychological measures."*

Emphasize that psychological testing is an accelerated search for personal truth. Teach them how to open to interpretations of data, such as being open to ALL possibilities. Use of their intuition is a key to interpretations that transform perspectives. Statistical interpretations lack impact on clients who see the results as "not me." Suggest the conscious dual-attention technique, which you would modify for their consumption. We can then have influence on a larger group of people. That's what Planetary Transformation is all about.

* * *

"Where shall we go today?"

We know where to take you today, just as you will know as you evolve. You will not have to wonder because you will know. We are eternally in the moment, knowing the state of things all the time. If you continue unifying with Us, you will know.

The present is all you have. The future builds on the present in that you go forward from where you are. Spending time worrying about the past is futile. If you accomplish what you can in the present, that is all you can do. Of course, Our presence in your consciousness makes quite a difference in how you benefit from the present as you move into the future. Since We are present in the unconsciousness of everyone, the task is to bring Our presence into their conscious minds.

It is Our presence that makes all transformation possible. Being "forever changed" depends on a conscious awareness of Our presence. Without Us, it would be overwhelming to attempt such a task. Because you have unified with Us, it is not overwhelming to Us. It will not be overwhelming to you either. Leave the work to Us. **All you have to do is become ever-accessible channels of Our energy on Earth. We will do the rest.** Notice how dual attention fits so well with this directive. Constant attunement is the secret to all We have told you over the past many years.

Jesus's purpose, as with the prophets of the Bible, was to bring to each person's consciousness an awareness of God's ever-presence. As you practice dual attention, We will engage more and more of your conscious awareness until We fill all of it with Our presence. This is what unifying with Us means. Then you will be fully in the present, making every second count toward your transformation.

"I clearly sensed Your direction a couple of times yesterday, but am having trouble focusing today."

Musing helps, so We will wait. We let you reflect a bit this morning so you could see where your mind goes without as much focusing energy as usual. Does this not support the concept of biological rhythms and motivation again for you? Though the concept is simple, it is effective in outlining how your motivation is in flux because of these built-in, regulated energy variations. We are in flux because of Our innate creativity.

Learning as discovery is Our favorite approach. Enlighten yourself when possible, and We will guide your pondering through dual attention to keep you from going too far afield. Conscious meandering is a creative act in which your mind is free to be led by Our influence toward new understandings that did not exist before. As an ever-widening path, this kind of meditation is a spiral of perspective expansion.

We are creativity itself, so your unity with Us ensures universal creativity as your experience. See the link between Our creativity and your manifestation. Again, our unity ensures both, which cannot be separated. Your creativity is Our creativity acting in support of you. The more We can act through you, the more universally creative you will be. Connecting through dual attention makes this possible. Is this not what you have been asking for over the many years of your life?

When your mind is free to roam, conscious exploration turns up the unexpected. This is where We pick up your mind's movement and guide it to new discoveries. We are the source of expansion. That is what creativity does. The universe appears to be expanding and not contracting because We are present as the expanding energy of love.

> "There is too much contraction in our beings. Help us release fear and replace it with your expanding energy of love."

That is just what We are doing every time your perspectives expand. Our new view of how the world operates releases fear-based limitations that fix you where you are. Freedom of movement then results, and even more discovery can be achieved, making you more secure and confident to take another step. Notice how self-reinforcing this process is.

The hard part is keeping up with the process by adjusting to each new change. Dual attention helps you with the pace. The faster you adjust, the freer you become, and the faster We can move. Adjustment time is the limiting factor.

With attitudes of willingness, adjustments to the new perceptions occur faster. This hastens the process because there is an absorption period required. Consider the important role that attitude plays in increasing the pace of the process. Attitude can either step on the gas, coast, or step on the brake. In many ways it is the controller.

Our team progress would not have been possible without willingness on your parts. That is what opening means: availability for experience that could not occur otherwise. Every possibility starts with openness and then converts into probabilities.

That is why the formula we gave you begins with open and expand. It starts with a conscious willingness to connect and to let Us do Our energy work. As you go through the day applying dual attention, remember that opening gives Us the freedom to do what is required for you to advance faster. We are in everything you do. Nothing happens in your lives without Our influence.

Are we still together?

"Definitely."

In one sense, all that you do is of consequence. However, what you do while consciously connected with Us is of much greater importance to your evolutions. It is a matter of how fast and how far you want to go. If your motivation is to go the limit – Ascension and Planetary Transformation – then stay tuned. If your motivation is anything less, it does not matter.

"Our motivation is to go the limit!"

Then listen constantly for Our guidance and We will see that you get there. The simple signal-light action-indicator from the past – red, yellow, and green – is gone for the moment. Such signals are for beginners in boot camp. You are past that, and are now required to sense Our intent in a different manner.

We are asking that you develop a degree of judgment equal to your advancement, appropriate to your "stations" on evolution's track. As you know, any natural developmental process occurs in steps or spurts. There is commonly the process of advance, plateau, advance, and plateau. The plateaus are your stations of consolidation and stabilization, getting ready for the next step, similar visually to an ancient step-pyramid. Use the plateau periods to assimilate your experiences of flourishing. Take a moment to absorb what you have done and let it become part of you. Stay tuned, and your feelings will guide you.

For those who maintain conscious connections with Us, it is possible to advance faster than in natural physical reality. We accelerate the consolidation process. Each assimilation step becomes shorter. Our intent is to advance you as quickly as possible. Consequently We will straighten your paths to help you arrive at the goal as soon as We can.

"We notice the impact of Your interventions and the momentum we feel."

You will experience your lives becoming more miraculous. There will be new high-quality occurrences that you are not used to experiencing. You will ask, "How did that happen?" We will answer, "Because of your conscious connection with LIFE, transformation of every aspect of your lives is in the wind." The direction is toward those transformations that are in your very best interests. When these events unfold, pay attention to your hearts and how grateful they are. **Natural appreciation is a signal of our connection**.

What have you done to deserve this? Plenty! The very practice of dual attention earns a person the privilege to experience Our energy. It is Our energy that brings joy. If you want joy, stick with Us. If you like what you have been experiencing recently, We are your team. You are getting a taste of what is to come.

> "We need to practice dual attention with our whole beings engaged, not just our thoughts. The difference is remarkable. Truth and timing – both goals we seek – elude us when our heart centers are not engaged.

We reiterate that nothing happens in your lives without Our influence, literally nothing. Boot camp sealed our connection, and we are merely elaborating on that connection as we go. Engaging your whole beings through dual attention speeds up the process. This permits us to do Our work much more completely and faster. You can sense the engagement down to your cores when it occurs. Open your entire beings as much as possible.

Let Us fill you with Our transforming energy through dual attention, which can change you as well as those with whom you come into contact. Depending on many factors, the effect is contagious, influencing everyone you deal with to a different extent. It is often subtle enough that it goes unrecognized consciously, but in fact it still occurs. The more convinced you are of this effect, the greater impact it will have.

What a good start for our ventures. Allow yourselves to absorb this new perspective and become convinced of the value of what We are saying. That conviction will "grease the rails."

You can see why each person is so important to Our goal of Planetary Transformation. Not only can the message We offer be effective, but its direct influence on others can be transforming. We want each of you to be in the presence of those who can influence the Earth as a whole. Every person's energy, which is Our energy working through them, powered by the contribution of dual attention to our unity, will change lives.

Go with Us, enjoying the ride, and "leave the driving to Us." We are the process experts, and you are the physical presences We need. This great combination can make us all successful. You are on the winning side, as strange as it can seem at times. Your power to win has changed character. Our energy ensures the victory now, not your attempts to manipulate the outcome. Our victory will be in the best interests of all Earth!

DUAL ATTENTION AND CONSCIOUSNESS SUMMARY

Choice is an important part of your conscious
effort to stay attuned.

Dual attention (DA) is a focus on the practical
while staying connected to universal energies.

DA is vital for continuous conscious connection
and unification with LIFE.

DA accelerates your evolution like no other technique.

With step-by-step direction, DA will transform your activities.

DA moves you out of the local flow into
the universal flow of LIFE.

The DA process reconstructs your unconscious mind.

LIFE'S connection with you has its basis in your
feelings and intuition.

In order to obtain humility and shun arrogance, your early
training may have diminished your sense of worthiness.

You deserve LIFE'S presence and partnership,
which LIFE cherishes.

Strength is more important now than anything else. Without
strength, manifestation and Ascension cannot materialize.

With DA, the strength of your connection and capacity for
manifestation increase.

Use DA to keep your connection open, awake or asleep.

Manifestation skills require macro energies that have
multidimensional scope.

Permit multidimensional energies to
assist you moment by moment through DA.

A conscious willingness to connect lets LIFE do
energy work within you.

The more LIFE can act through you,
the more universally creative you will be.

Using DA, let LIFE fill you with Their transforming energy.

Your DNA in every cell can be changed to bring about
preparation for Ascension.

PART NINE

DUAL ATTENTION AND ULTIMATE UNITY

"We yearn to open and expand for the unity you promise. Besides practicing dual attention, which we are doing, is there anything else that could help us?

The ultimate unity We intend comes from higher-quality opening, expanding, and connecting experiences. Then following depends on receiving direction by query or suggestion. Merely practicing dual attention is important, and the higher the quality of your practice – connecting without distractions – the further you will go. A fleeting dual attention serves a longer purpose, but will not advance you quickly enough. Can you devote some time to just open and expand and nothing else? You can arrange other times for questions and answers, which are like the icing on the cake. You may find this tedious to do for a while, but it will pay major dividends all around.

"We can."

Without adequate opening and expanding, our connection is compromised. When our connection is compromised, noise disrupts the quality of connection and much of the value is lost. **The lifeblood of unity runs through the quality of connection, enhanced by dual attention, but established by adequate opening (willingness) and expanding (inclusion).** To have unity with Us, you will be required to become as all-encompassing as We are. Our love and joy expand until they include all there is.

Opening and expanding to include all there is allows you to know what the intent of creation is. Then you can use everything appropriately for its intended purpose, which decreases overall distortion. This is the unity We propose.

LIFE has a place for everything that is – an appropriate time and place for anything you can imagine. It is the misappropriation of any part of everything that creates distortion of love and joy. LIFE knows what is intended through every creative action. If what is created is used inappropriately – used against its intended purpose – this is a distortion of intent. Inappropriateness is a distortion that can self-multiply, just as appropriateness is self-reinforcing. Becoming unified with LIFE, cooperating with the intent of creation, decreases the possibility of distortion.

Imagine all the people on Earth having the same intent as creation. Talk about Planetary Transformation! Billions of souls connected with LIFE, collaborating with the same intent – now that is unity on a large scale! The intent of creation, as we have said before, is to entertain all possibilities while considering the highest interests of all concerned.

* * *

"Just letting ourselves dream is difficult because the power we assign to the present overwhelms our visions."

Your visions have to become possible within the present – not just future yearnings, but here, right now. Superimpose your dreams on the present while living concurrently with both. Again, dual attention is a useful tool for this advancement.

Draw yourselves toward your dreams, constantly using their attraction. You can literally pull your present experiences into your dreams and transform what exists into what can be. Then permit your dreams to be unlimited resources. The power of your dreams creates its own possibilities. But the only dependence that works is complete reliance on our unity.

First you must be transformed by Our presence in order to transform anyone else. This is described as "being filled with the Holy Spirit" in the Bible – an ongoing, increasing experience in which you advance toward becoming your dreams. This describes the essence of your roles and the empowerment that makes you effective.

* * *

"Should we be formulating priorities or values that reflect the intent of creation?"

That will come in time. Right now the focus is on being willing to cooperate with the intent of creation and its source – LIFE. As with the training of children, attitudes and behaviors come first, then values and beliefs follow. The order here is willingness first, then reasoning later.

For most people, intuition – knowing something without discovering or perceiving it – functions actively in their real experience. Intuition is one of Our favored modes for training.

"Thank you again for this important clarity."

To repeat, know that We have at our disposal all that We have created, which is everything, including money. We can stimulate your income from many diverse sources. So your aligning with Us puts you in position for manifesting income from these diverse sources. Continuing to unify with Us is the secret to your success in manifesting money, or healing, or anything else.

Notice We are repeating what We have said many times before. Nothing We say is said lightly. **We want an alliance on a continual basis – connections that never sleep, knowing that never rests.**

This repetition is intended to help motivate you to devote your time and energies to our joint efforts. Dual attention is designed for this. Our creativity, to which you have access, is prolific. Manifesting should be no problem whatsoever as you align more and more with our creativity.

> "We want continuing conversations, leading to ultimate unity with You."

Your comment mirrors Our intent. We are present in all that you live, so let's have continuing conversations. We are not going anywhere else, and We are continually accessible. So tune in with dual attention. Tune in by experiencing the great vortex at all times, whatever you might be doing. It lifts you out of the mundane and fills your experiences with meaning. The energy that results empowers your efforts to help others as well.

With dual attention, We are only a thought away, and We prefer being part of all you do in order to prepare you for Planetary Transformation. This is one way to speed things up. Since you have been asking about increasing the pace of your evolutions, We waited for you to perceive the possibility of broadening Our conversations with you. It's now up to you to bring this new unifying approach to fruition. We will keep Our end of the bargain if you will keep your end. Just turn your attention toward Us and We will respond.

Your dedication to greater access through meditation enables Us to work all the faster toward unity. Your preparation for Our influence determines how quickly we can advance. That is why the dual-attention technique is so valuable to use at this time. You are capable of maintaining dual attention and can develop this skill through use. **We do not ask anything of you that you are not already capable of doing**. As you master the skill that We speak of, the emphasis on the next skill comes to the fore. Look at these skills as building a repertoire that will serve you from now on.

With stability in mind, focus your intent and practice. Such sturdiness has a substantial passion associated with it in the form of conviction. By establishing solid foundations from which to operate, you help accelerate your progress toward unity.

These developments could not have taken place without you both preparing yourselves through meditation and dual attention. As chaotic as your development seems, you are making headway toward ultimate unity.

"That is very encouraging."

Just as someone would lead you if you were blindfolded, your intent leads you in the right direction, feeling your way and listening for Our voice with dual attention. We clear the way to protect you because We do not encourage you to hurt yourselves. At the same time We watch possibilities turn into probabilities, matching the energy synchronicities necessary for events to occur with the best timing for the highest benefit of all concerned.

Remember once again that nothing happens to you now without Our intervention. Every event that occurs is a training ground for the Planetary Transformation roles you will both play. See every event as an opportunity for learning something that will aid you later. There is nothing frivolous about Our operations. While encountering circumstances now, imagine yourselves already in roles of the future. This will make current events more meaningful in the scheme of things.

By using dual attention to stay in tune, you do not need time to become "acclimatized" to Us when you meditate; you are already there.

"We are not sure how well established our connection is with You."

You have asked that any communication between us be clearly and objectively Our voice speaking to you, not you imagining Us speaking to you. We are making every attempt to keep the connection energized, operative, and free-flowing. Since it serves all of us, it is Our intent to have this connection working well.

"Why do we still have doubts about it?"

You tend to be impatient with Our long pauses before responding to you, even though We are taking the time necessary to provide the best reply for the situation. Would you rather that We be reckless in Our answers to meet your immediacy?

"No."

Then you must be willing to give Us the time necessary to respond appropriately. In some cases it is immediate, but in other cases you are not ready for Our instant response, so We must wait for you to get ready. You see, the response We offer must be in the highest interests of all concerned.

Your state of readiness for ultimate unity determines what is in your best interests. Any time you spend getting into more advanced states of readiness is to all of our advantages. Meditating for no reason except to ready yourself is worthwhile at this stage of your development. That is why at times We have nothing to say to you that is as important as the readiness you gain by being in connection with Us. It is the conscious connection that frees Us to advance your readiness. Think of the percentages. How much of your waking or conscious time is spent in conscious connection with Us using dual attention?

"Maybe two or three hours out of some seventeen are spent consciously keeping the connection going."

Well, there you have the picture that We see. Does this represent your intent or motivation?

"I don't think so."

More quality time spent practicing dual attention will help you change, since change depends on your making it happen. Think of dual attention as having a connection earphone in your ear at all times. You never take it out, waking or sleeping, and it is waterproof.

"That is a helpful image."

Notice how easily this can work when you use both sides of your brain simultaneously. This will speed up the unifying process. Is that not what you asked for?

We continue to harp on the dual-attention technique because it serves many purposes for you and for Us. Stay in tune with Us using dual attention, and the connection will not fade; rather your feelings of unity will grow in intensity and meaning.

"Connecting with You throughout the day makes it easier to formally meditate when we have time."

Quieting yourself makes Our presence more obvious. While connecting with Us, notice that counseling with clients has a quieting and focusing influence on you. The more you are channels of Our energy, the more natural Our connection with you and your sense of our unity will be.

That is one reason for emphasizing that Charlie become fluent in Our communication with her. Writing a novel has aided her in connecting to Us, with Mattie and Gabriel as her guides. It is just a matter of intent and practice, because you have been out of the habit since you were young children, when conversing with Us was natural. **The current environment on Earth is not conducive to your connecting with Us. That is why it takes effort to reopen the conversation, since a connection with Us is not encouraged in your everyday lives. Have you ever seen it on the front page of any newspaper?**

"We are so easily distracted."

Anticipation on your part – waiting to hear what significant information We have to share or just expecting Us to speak –

enhances the connection and eases distraction. Even in your anxious distraction, orient yourselves to listen for the still, small voice. Notice, even now, how Our voice and your thoughts are blending to be one. Your confidence develops through strengthening our connection.

Since We are the instigators of all circumstances you encounter, make your daily lives as meditations. We have an interest in all situations.

Purpose is one of Our themes, so no situation arises without Our influence. Knowing this permits you to become involved in every situation with Our ongoing guidance. **Nothing happens to you without a bigger purpose being involved.** We have spoken about how simplification of your lives permits more of a long-term focus on ultimate unity with Us.

It is to your advantage to know the complexity that you are willing to live with and to monitor developments as they occur, asking Us when you are uncertain. Knowing what you can manage is to your advantage in the roles you are to play. So do not compare yourselves with others. Look inside, where We keep you advised. Successful management of just the right amount of complexity builds strength and confidence.

Dual attention allows you to ask Us, at any time, about adding something to or subtracting something from your already complex lives. Since We are responsible for bringing some of these complexities into your lives, We are hesitant to provide general rules for this matter. Moreover, because flexibility must be honored in order to take advantage of opportunities as they arise, moving forward gradually seems wiser.

* * *

The many personalities of past meditations appear and bring joy in their wake. They are dancing around us in celebration.

"How do we become harmonious with these universal energies?"

Ponder them, include them, let them reveal themselves to you. The personalities that We presented represent qualities of universal energies. Start there and use your familiarity with these many expressions of Us: Alexander, Babaji, Lang, the Man in Grey, and Saint Vincent.

Babaji speaks.

The universal flow is joyful, just as you see with me. Celebrate its joy as it displaces your local flow and remains undistorted by the frailty of human beings. The more you know about the Cosmos and its characteristics, the more you will appreciate the energy of the universal flow and choose to remain immersed.

First there is preparation, and then manifestation follows. They are both essential steps in the order of evolution. Today you are being prepared. Tomorrow you will manifest. Engage in the phase in which you find yourself. This soothes the panic that otherwise arises.

You cannot skip the preparation to get to manifestation. Permit the preparation to advance and manifestation will occur sooner. Distraction slows preparation. Focus on the models you use, Babaji (me) and the Man in Grey. We are real, living models, alive in the universal flow. Be there!

Multiple dimensions are not a new concept for you. Notice how you cross dimensions to connect with Us. You have learned what it takes to move back and forth between dimensions. That is why I, the Man in Grey, and the rest of LIFE, are so real to you. The players accumulate as you experience crossing more dimensions of LIFE – an infinitely multidimensional existence. With some you feel more affinity than with others. All are expanding parts of your experience.

* * *

Noise from immersion in the local flow drowns out universal flow. Remain centered in the universal flow, on the periphery of local flow. Immersion in the universal flow is the better choice for you. You have been applying the universal flow to your lives every time you invoke the formula We gave you, except that now you are conscious of doing it.

Thanks to those energies assisting you, you are not the same! Wherever you are, the situation is filled with your supporting cast of universal players. Your journey is alone, but not lonely if you remain in the universal flow. Always alone, never lonely. Be there fully. Enjoy the crowds. They are enjoying you, with energy and respect. They are clapping with support and enthusiasm. Hear them. Babaji and the Man in Grey and the others are very present. **Admit Them as your team**.

Depend on yourselves to develop new styles. You have been given various models, all expressions of LIFE. Each one offers different skills and emphasis. Babaji offers a joyous outlook and magical creative ability. The Man in Grey offers quiet knowing, steadfastness of duty, and problem-solving, with a soft, military discipline. Lang offers networking, interpreting, and communication skills. Though still in the background, others have faded in their relevance to you at this time, and more may appear.

Apparent or not, you have a continually renewing cadre of caring assistants who serve as mentors with universal skills. They come and go as you change – a dynamic process of multidimensional evolution. You "travel" much more than you realize, as do They. Fortunately for Us, there is no here or there. There is only now.

* * *

"Is our general opening and expanding enough for ultimate unity?"

You are points of light in the universal body of Christ that remain lit at all times because you have given your assent to our partnership in Planetary Transformation – ultimate unity. That is the "general openness and expansion" that you are asking about. Such points of light draw Our energy at all times because we are connected in a general way as well as in a specific way. This connection is a continuous communication channel that is responsive in both directions. Changes within you, of which you are not consciously aware, take place all the time.

Seeing the colors in the great vortex alerts you to the shifts that Our energy is regularly creating within you. Our work never stops, and your changes are always progressing, but in the background, which is slower than in the foreground.

To bring them to the foreground requires your conscious involvement. Your attention to the transformation process concentrates the effects of Our work, focusing and multiplying it through active participation rather than passive acceptance. Assertive involvement enlivens your receptors, drawing Our energy to you. Remember the woman who touched the hem of Jesus's garment. That was conscious involvement – an active, intentional effort on her part to draw His energy her way.

To accelerate your advance toward ultimate unity, bring your intentions to the foreground as much as possible. Open and expand through dual attention in an active, intentional process.

* * *

"If You are all possibilities, why must we, who are parts of You, have these many experiences? Aren't we already complete?"

We have thrown choice into the mix. On Earth there is nothing but experience. Simple as well as complex events require choices on your part. Possibilities are constantly mixing, blending to form a flow of probabilities that enfold you. Remember the clouds of the sky and how they move.

People live out the notion of all possibilities, making choices that can move them toward Our intent for creation. All that We encourage is in the highest interests of everyone, Our primary motivation for action on Earth.

Remember, the now is all there is, and is forever changing. Memory, as part of consciousness, gives you the capacity to retain your experiences and permits you to create the artificial concept of time – past, present, and future. It is best for you to move with the irregular flow of probabilities, taking advantage of them as they develop rather than moving with the regular flow of artificial time.

Evolutionary acceleration is accomplished by immersing yourselves in Our energy as much as possible. **We prefer the speed of your evolutions to exceed the pace of planetary development.**

Step into the universal flow like sponges, absorbing Our energy throughout your beings, while advancing toward our ultimate unity. Can you see the purpose for opening and expanding as a formula of significance?

* * *

As you use dual attention in your waking lives, ask about everything! Even when falling asleep, train yourselves to be in dual-attention mode. This allows Us to work 24/7 in bringing about Ascension as a real possibility.

When people prepare for Ascension, they must know that it involves cell transformation, which dual attention encourages. We will modify everyone's energies in such a way that their cells are reinvigorated, rebuilding their bodies into new forms. Their cells await Our instruction via energy signals with the intelligence that We have bestowed on them. The cells will respond by continuing to do their magic.

"What do you mean by 'new forms'?"

Notice the halos in older paintings. Are they not symbolic of a higher energy? As never before, ordinary people will shine with the glow of Our LIFE force. Our energy present in them is what draws others to them without their knowing why. Changes will take place within them to bring this state to fruition. An emphasis on skills first should be in the context of increasing ultimate unity with Us, as well as the development of this Christ-like state of being.

The mind of Christ worked this way. His dual-attention skills were so highly developed that He was always in two places at once, with the physical as well as the LIFE that sustains it. This is the way We want everyone to become!

When someone gets to that point, it can be difficult to discriminate between the guidance and their physical experience, because the two blend completely. Because of our ultimate unity, they feel charged with Our energy, and creative manifestation is natural.

"That is a tall order!"

It is a tall order, but attainable if the person is operating in ultimate unity with Us. They will manifest Our energy in as pure a form as possible for human beings. Training and transformation are both necessary for these roles. That is why this time has been so intense for you. We have been providing training for the future roles you will play.

Everyone will be purified! By this We mean that distracting elements will be removed so that their presence will accurately represent the intent of Our energy, expressed in each circumstance. They will be the ambassadors of Our intent for the Earth. Ambassadors accurately represent their country's intent. Their "home and country" is with Us.

DUAL ATTENTION AND
ULTIMATE UNITY SUMMARY

Nothing happens to you without a bigger purpose involved.

The order is willingness first, then reasoning later.

Meditating for no reason except to
ready yourself is worthwhile.

LIFE does not ask anything of you that
you are not already capable of doing.

Think of dual attention as having a connection earphone in
your ear at all times. You never take it out,
waking or sleeping, and it is waterproof.

It helps if you look forward to connection with Us.

Anticipation before connecting improves
its quality and advances you faster.

Continuing to unify with LIFE is the secret to success in
manifesting money, healing, or anything else.

The ultimate unity LIFE intends comes from high-quality
opening, expanding, and connecting.

Your following depends on asking questions or
receiving suggestions from LIFE.

LIFE wants an alliance on a continuing basis – connections that
never sleep; knowing that never rests.

Bring your intention to the foreground as much as possible,
which advances you toward ultimate unity.

Remember, the now is all there is,
and is forever changing.

When you prepare for Ascension,
dual attention encourages DNA transformation.

It is better to be in the irregular flow of probabilities than
moving with the regular flow of artificial time.

LIFE intends to speed up everyone's evolution to exceed the
current pace of planetary development over eons.

PART TEN

DUAL ATTENTION
AND TIMELESS FLOW

You have discovered timeless timing, a trademark of Our approach. By remaining in the timeless flow of Our energy, you draw probabilities toward you. Dual attention must be steady enough to stabilize the energy attraction. This is the secret.

> "I watched the circulation of the clouds. Guided by the weather, there is a slow but steady movement within ambient conditions. Like the clouds, are You guiding us by the probabilities that are in our best interests?"

At this time you have all of LIFE in support of your actions. It may be clearer to think in terms of the energy supporting your intent. Be sure to specialize in the energy-moment and your quality of living will be changed forever. Your intent can collaborate with the energy-moment. Unity with Us means unity with the energy-moment. We are the energy that can see when fluctuations match your intent.

Observe the importance of your intent in this context. See how it works in conjunction with the timeless universal energy flow. Stay in tune to be available on short notice for a shift in emphasis and to take advantage of the support that exists in the energy-moment; it is Our energy, which includes all of LIFE as you experience it on Earth.

> "If we exist in a sea of LIFE energy that permeates all of creation, are we not connected all of the time,

without being conscious of it? If so, we cannot *NOT* be connected. So dual attention reinforces our conscious awareness of the energy sea that sustains us."

Yes. This is an idea that can advance your dual-attention success. As you feel more at home in the eternal "energy sea" surrounding you, step consciously out of your four-dimensional orientation into a perspective of ultimate unity with Us.

This makes your connecting with Us much more direct than you had thought. The key is turning your consciousnesses to Us, which is an act of choice. There is no real separation from Us. Through conscious connection with Us, your power levels are stepped up. It will make for easier connection, and dual attention will be more effective.

"Sometimes we feel as if we are in limbo."

Everyone is in limbo when they move from one place to another in their individual evolutions. Get used to it! The insecurity you feel is more from your spiritual advancement than your physical circumstances. As advancement takes place, it supersedes your concerns about your physical circumstances. Your priorities are changing.

Circumstances provide opportunities for choices, actions, and their consequences to be experienced. The results of your choices and actions have consequences built in. All circumstances are opportunities to correct those choices and actions that are not in your highest interests. This combination of choices, actions, and consequences is what makes learning from experience necessary for self-forgiveness to be effective.

Therefore focus on those possibilities that are in your best interests. We are active in all possibilities. Only those possibilities that serve you are considered. We do

not punish anyone with potentialities that work against their best interests. Humans do well enough punishing themselves.

> "I just realized how involved opening is. It embraces many different avenues of information flow (the six senses), different means (various people), different states (awake, asleep, preoccupied), and different circumstances (quiet, chaotic). Utter complexity!"

For dual attention to work, your awareness must stay available in every way and under all conditions. Turn Us on and use Us as a GPS system guiding you at all times. Pauses are acceptable. We will present a voice that you recognize. Look for other information coming your way as well. Attempt to recognize it all.

An Easter egg hunt is a good image for the dual-attention process. "I know the egg is here in my presence. Where could it be hiding?" How to search is part of your training, an excellent practice to hone your skills for staying tuned in!

You asked for Our guidance, direction, and renewed vision. Here is a way to have clarity that serves you as you work. We provide the vision for the effort you supply. You truly become Our hands at work in the world. Without your conscious collaboration with Us, Our designs cannot become reality on Earth.

Your conscious alliance with Us gives Us channels for the transmission of Our intent. With this in mind, your capacity for conscious choice becomes essential to Our long-range plans. Dual attention requires the presence of conscious choice at all times, which gives Us continuous channels for transmission of Our energy. Do you see how Our mission can be accelerated through the application of this simple technique?

* * *

Master your awareness of the universal, timeless flow. Recognize it as familiar energy, even more so than the local flow. See the local distortions clearly and move away from them toward the undistorted universal flow. Feelings will guide you.

To reconnect consciously and immediately with Us when you become distracted, listen to the rhythms of your hearts and of your breaths. These rhythms can remind you of your humanness and our connectedness. At the same time they facilitate dual attention.

There are also subtle vibrations of energy within your bodies, like subdued musical rhythms, that are indicators of Our energy-sharing. It is easy to sway internally with these rhythms and sense the connection we have. The still, small voice is related to your inner rhythms.

* * *

"For reasons not clear to me, I feel angst this morning. My mind is wandering aimlessly. Focusing is difficult, and dual attention is spotty. I feel as if I have been beaten up. What is going on?

Rise above the practical details and maintain the larger view that demonstrates where we are headed. Do not let practical details mislead your emotions. Do not permit the absurdity of the local flow to bog you down. Fear stops you in your tracks and leaves you without a compass. Your compass is Our energy and the grand purpose that We champion.

We are not the source of your fear and insecurity. Trusting in Us excludes fear and insecurity. Trust is opposed to fear and insecurity.

From time to time You may be required to recommit to the trust We represent. This is one of those times. Stay with Us and your angst will dissolve. Our connection is your lifeline. Strengthen it with dual attention. Master the skill and times of recommitment will become unnecessary.

"We lean on You heavily."

Because there is no better or faster way, this is the way We like it. To know that We are truly your saving grace is essential to where we are headed. And make no mistake, we are headed to the "big time!" Hang on!

You will look back on these times as the crucible that prepared you. Take a sacred view of all that is happening at this time. It is not punishment, rather training. You asked for a fast transformation. Here it is, speeded up, demanding that appropriate perspectives be maintained while you are being renewed. Dual-attention techniques will help you through these times, so be sure to engage them for perspective.

"You have exhorted us to focus on essentials, and to not use our energy for any other reason."

Essentials derive from an emphasis on unity with Us. As We have said, unity means you operate continually with the mind of Christ, directly knowing what is essential to your purposes at any given time. The mind of Christ functions with undisturbed dual attention since it is a human example of Our presence on Earth. Connection is complete, timeless, with no interference. You are here and there at the same time. Notice that here and there are the same anyway. Before long, with eyes open or closed, **here is all there is**. The sooner the better.

This is your reality check. Under these conditions, essentials rise to the top of your priority lists. To know what your essentials consist of, stay attuned to Our presence in your lives. Ask and know. Know without asking. **Just know!**

"Our focus seesaws back and forth. We find it difficult to live our physical lives fully, while at the same time we are living our universal lives fully."

Yes, and without going to extremes either way. You simultaneously have bodies, in Earth form, and you have spirits, Our energy. Does not that combination speak to the importance of mastering dual attention? Give equal value to each. You are learning to value both in the challenges that you face. An ear to each voice provides the balance of value that We intend. In this great experiment, neither is less important to Us.

Your keen-observer role is evolving, permitting you to respond when it is important while you remain on the periphery of local circumstances. From that vantage point you can reside in Our energy while interacting in the stream of life, keeping a foot in both places. This exemplifies dual attention.

* * *

"Please comment on the increasingly chaotic time in our local and international world."

The current chaos and confusion is for the benefit of all, and you are caught up in it because you live on Earth at this time. The circumstances are not personal, though since We intend it to be in the best interests of everyone's development, it can serve you as well. See what you can learn from this impersonal moment.

Within this context, simplicity, not confusion, is the order of the day. "Simple" will serve you best from an energy standpoint. Effortlessness is welcome. Enjoy the relief when you view your lives this way with no gingerbread or trappings.

Be sure to practice dual attention until it becomes automatic. Your conscious awareness can be trained to lean toward dual attention at all times. With the fruits of this pattern becoming habit, your dual attention will displace other concerns. Sense the feeling of unity more than the thought of it. Experience the bond. Make it tangible. Go beyond the principle of unity to knowing the feeling of being one with Us.

"We want to experience unity with You more intensely than we experience our bodies!"

You are exercising a truth that will set you free. Become committed to the truth of your origins, with refreshingly new perceptions that **emphasize forever**. Using dual attention to open and expand all of the time, keep your focus on Us! We will guide and direct everything you do, taking one step at a time.

Remember that **your home is with Us**. Your house is just a house. Meld with Our creative power and feel it available to you. Make it your home away from home and be comfortable with it at all times, in all places. Be in it rather than viewing it from a distance. Experience it constantly, even when you do the most menial tasks. Never leave its presence!

All becomes simpler when you join with Our energy. Because you are home, the need to be shrewd or artificial dissolves as you consciously approach Our presence with expanding openness. You can be your real selves at home. That is what We want for everyone. Remind yourselves constantly of the real connection that never fails. Let it become your dominant conscious experience.

* * *

It is becoming more important to be connected no matter what you are doing. Energy movement has increased its pace. Probabilities collect and disperse more quickly, necessitating connection at all times in order to take advantage of their influence.

Energy flux is what We know, so Our guidance can be timely and direct if you stay consciously connected. Availability is the key to receiving Our guidance. We know that you do not want to miss anything.

Take a new look at your lives. Along with the evolutionary struggles each person goes through, improvements will result. Be faithful to the changing evolutionary pace you have taken on. Take the time to review the improvements that have occurred or else they will be missed. Encourage each other, and celebrate your accomplishments together.

"Matters of growth take time. Do we have time?"

Even with the pressure of time running out as a motivation to act, sometimes you are not ready. Matters of growth are to be achieved and assimilated for stability. Whether earlier or later, the time must be taken, and it is better earlier than at the last moment.

"How do we act earlier?"

Remain open to the fast-changing possibilities using dual attention. You can no longer wait for chances to sit and meditate. We must communicate on the run now. Develop your dual-attention skills by practicing everywhere.

Nobody need know what you are doing, but they will be impressed by the intimate wisdom you bring forth under various circumstances. Recall the wisdom that flowed during a recent counseling session. Psychological tests served as triggers for our connection to occur in the midst of other activities taking place at the same time.

Because we are linked and aware of fast-changing possibilities, you will begin to foresee what is coming and prepare earlier. This awareness precedes the need so that you can respond earlier than at the last moment.

The value of your knowledge base is no longer a product of formal classes. It is a flow of Our inspiration necessary at that moment. Formal classes are required to fulfill regulations, but the real eye-opening wisdom for living can flow directly from Us. Does it get any better than that?

"How can we recognize possibilities that are in our best interests?

Watch your feelings – a useful guidance system. Are you attracted or repelled? Are you inspired or let down? Is there a compelling pull toward the opportunity? Is expansion rather than contraction part of the prospect? These are feelings more than thoughts, although the two can combine. You have an altar and the great vortex to use, and there are beings ready to assist you from around the Cosmos. All you have to do is ask.

* * *

"Why must we endure dark nights of the soul?

Honesty, sincerity, and commitment will take you through these dark places. If you want nothing but the very best that We have to offer, you can't lose! Maintain this approach and you will win the prize.

You may find that persevering is a challenge. Strength builds from maintaining. Endurance and inspiration are powerful motivations to achieve. While you endure, We provide the inspiration, which is a true team effort. Expect this inspiration; that is Our power available to you. Dual attention is a channel for on-the-spot inspiration, and inspiration in a difficult situation is powerful medicine. Stay in the bright daylight of Our inspiration at all times, and there will be fewer dark nights of the soul.

* * *

"Which is more important, dual attention or formal meditation?"

Do what you are able to do. However you contact us, leave the door open at all times for interaction with Us. Dual attention is applied energy. Formal meditation is an opportunity for assimilation of the energy We share with you. It is less busy, permitting digestion and incorporation of Our energy. You need both understanding and practice of the new perspectives. Meditation together with dual attention round out your evolution. So open up and practice both!

* * *

"How can we recognize the universal timeless flow?"

In meditation, you leave a local awareness to focus on the connection with Us. Doing so, you experience the universal energy of our connection. Afterward, you add a local awareness to the universal consciousness you have just experienced. These are the two flows We speak about.

The universal timeless flow has more welcoming source energy than the local assaulting flow. By virtue of being human, you tend to focus on the local flow even though the preferred focus for you is the universal flow, a more nourishing one.

Like an observer on a train watching the scenery passing by, think of tapping in to a flow that already exists rather than having to create it. The flow can be as small or as large in scope as you wish; the larger the scope, the more universal the flow. Bring the influence of the larger scope to the smaller flow.

Your guidance comes from the universal flow with a maximum of clarity and a minimum of distortion. Dual attention provides you with a contrasting awareness of how distorted and misleading the local flow can be.

Those immersed in the local flow are misdirected by the distortion of source energy. The biblical temptation of Christ clearly describes the distortion of His local flow. A variety of human emotions can warp the local flow.

Human distortion of source energy can be devilish in its effects. **Evil becomes possible through human choice when a choice**

is not in the highest interests of everyone concerned. This is choice outside of the universal flow, which explains why local and universal probabilities differ.

Even though your life history contains distortions, by staying connected We bring to the fore any distortion that still exists. Distortions are contrary to truth. This awareness permits you to clear the distortion and respond more readily and accurately to truth as it appears. We are truth and creativity in their most complete and purest forms. As long as We guide you, truth is prominent and you can count on your emotions to reflect Our direction. This accelerates your evolution.

Immersion in the universal flow minimizes distorted choices. If you know the universal flow intimately, you can gauge the choices you make as being supportive of your own well-being.

You exist in both the universal and local flows, but are nurtured by only one, the universal flow. Creating an undistorted human experience requires returning to a greater focus on the universal energy flow.

* * *

"How do we ask the universal helpers for assistance?

The Man in Grey appeared to you early in your conscious awareness of Our presence. Dual attention is the secret to the Man in Grey, who has mastered conscious connection at all times. This is an example of Our knowing what is in your best interests, a taste of the universal support We offer you.

Whether you are in the fast lane or the slow lane of evolutionary change, know that helpers are here, available and ready to act. Invite the "momentum specialists" to bring about knowing within you, and whatever else you need. They will prevent your slowing to a standstill. Momentum is Their hallmark. They are the movers and shakers of the

Cosmos, and are able to guide you. Movement is toward Our goal of Planetary Transformation.

Ask for Their assistance even though you might be reluctant. When you see what they can do, you will rely on them more. Those of you moving in the fast lane need all the help you can get. Much is required of you. So take advantage of the offer and incorporate the help available. Invite the momentum specialists to join your journey.

* * *

"Our listening needs to improve, especially under duress."

That is true! As you are beginning to understand, Our purposes are multilayered. We prepare you for just the right timing. If what We say is ignored or postponed, the timing is thrown off and the meaning for you is lost. This puts you behind the eight-ball, which requires a more complex recovery.

We know probabilities, so We can operate in the clearest and simplest mode. Getting to know the probabilities does the same for you, simplifying your lives, especially during turbulent times.

"We would like that."

Your opening and expanding this morning brought you closer to acquainting yourselves with the probabilities that We know. Using an inclusive process, you can engage all possibilities that are in the highest interests of everyone. Probabilities arise from this approach. **Timing is crucial for taking advantage of the way energies form into probabilities. Receive Our assessment of the existing possibilities through knowing, which provides you with the resulting probabilities. Knowing combines the probabilities with timing.**

Systems like astrology are attempts to reach the same conclusion – the marriage of probabilities and timing. Systems can provide hints but do not replace the smoothness of knowing. Through your past explorations of many systems, some more efficient than others, you evidenced an interest in knowing. We are providing the best solution in answer to your search. Act on Our lead and you will be in the flow of universal probabilities and timing, which command the outcomes of your lives!

With knowing as your method, We can provide a lead in every circumstance that occurs. Knowing is Our immediate connection with you. Dual attention encourages knowing. Meditation encourages knowing. Prayer encourages knowing.

You must be prepared to take the path less traveled at times, because local probabilities differ from universal probabilities. Elicit your curiosity at these times and explore the strangeness of the path. **In the end, opt for the larger view, which encompasses more effective options.**

Do not let your past place restrictions on your future. In the past you have stumbled into knowing. Now you can intentionally go there. Practice going there. The future from here is unlimited. Allow yourselves to slip into it. Take a refreshing view and renew your perspectives, which free possibilities to fit into place. Be refreshed in spirit, ready for the next great adventure, which is just around the corner. Be open to the universal flow of Our energy, which can transport you to the places prepared for you. Dual attention ensures your arrival!

Rely on the timeless flow. We will get it right. Hence you will get it right.

DUAL ATTENTION
AND TIMELESS FLOW SUMMARY

You exist in a sea of LIFE energy that permeates
all of creation; you cannot NOT be connected.

Circumstances provide opportunities to experience choices,
actions, and their consequences.

Learning from these three opportunities
makes self-forgiveness possible.

To reconnect consciously and immediately with LIFE,
listen to the rhythms of your heart and breath.

There are subtle vibrations of energy in your body,
like subdued musical rhythms,
which are indicators of LIFE'S energy-sharing.

You simultaneously have a body (Earth form) and a spirit
(LIFE'S energy).

Listening to each voice provides the balance that LIFE intends.
In this great experiment, both are important to you.

Remember that your home is with LIFE.

Encourage each other, and celebrate your
accomplishments together.

Because you are linked with LIFE and aware of
fast-changing possibilities, you will begin to
foresee what is coming and prepare earlier.

Human distortion of source energy can be
devilish in its effects. Evil becomes possible through
human choice when it is not in the
highest interests of everyone concerned.

LIFE prepares you with just the right timing.
If what LIFE says is ignored or postponed,
the timing is thrown off and the meaning for you is lost.

Timing is crucial for taking advantage of the way
energies are formed into probabilities.
Knowing combines the probabilities with timing.

You must be prepared to take the path less traveled at times,
because local probabilities and universal probabilities differ.

Do not let your past place restrictions on your future.

PART ELEVEN

MULTIDIMENSIONAL ENERGY

"Are there any other skills to develop along the way?"

Yes. One is multidimensional flexibility – to be consciously willing and able to go anywhere, anytime. In other words, welcome all energies that make up LIFE to be present within you. Opening and expanding produces this ability. Surprised?

In addition, universal principles must be brought to bear on everyday life, which then transforms local life into universal LIFE. A four-dimensional experience is not enough for this job, making a multidimensional exposure to LIFE important.

Planetary Transformation will bring a new Earth into being, an Earth that is in agreement with itself. This new harmony will have a rippling effect on the energy of the entire Cosmos. LIFE is holistic, a unity. When one part changes, the whole is affected. Connections exist throughout LIFE that transmit change. LIFE is interconnected and unified.

Energy exists alone, with all its qualities – potential, kinetic, etc. Process (like evolution) requires a time concept. Earth life is a process-oriented life. There are stages of existence on Earth and its related universe created especially for that purpose.

A multidimensional matrix of connections is available to you, like tributaries from the main source. When We talk about Us, We mean Us in the cosmic sense of all energies available and expressed in creation.

Coming from all corridors, assistance will arrive in the strangest of ways. Be available to it, because the energies that respond are specialists in the very need that exists at the time. Capable of resolving whatever issue is prominent at the time, They are your emergency assistants.

When We were first formally introduced to Kelly by Dan, he experienced Us in many forms, each having a different personality and name, identified separately from each other. He felt comfortable with an assortment of energies interacting with him. Then We coalesced into one central energy for a while. Now you are clear that these are the energies of creation, all expressions of God the Creator, or LIFE, all unified with a central purpose.

> "We accept what they have to offer with new enthusiasm. We are turning more to the universal flow for perspective and for the benefit of all concerned."

The multidimensional character of Our energy broadens your perspectives of all possibilities, expanding your vision of Us. **Be prepared for the unexpected. Accept the unusual, even the weird yet plausible. Your journeys within the universal flow reveal a side of the plausible that you would not expect. When you are surprised, look for the identifying energy that We represent for the confirmation within you. If you did not know Us, you would tend to reject what comes your way. Just know that We send only those who deserve to be there, having earned the right, as strange as it may seem. Do your best to accommodate those who appear. Those who stay benefit from being there. Jesus loved the fringe elements of society and drew them close to Him. Do the same.**

You have established a connection with Us that will not weaken and will only strengthen with use. Being distant from Us is a lie, since We are always present within you. Those who create fear also preach your being remote from Us, as in your early days. There is no such thing except in the minds of those people. **Even when seemingly abandoned, you are not. The same power that is present at confident times is also present at fearful times. Count on Us more and you will prosper, flourishing in the way you intend. Stay in the knowing rather than the logical. The knowing embraces the unexpected and the creative.**

* * *

"We want to take every opportunity to further develop our ultimate unity."

That is good to hear since time is of the essence. Once again, new entities will appear to guide you from time to time. Do not be surprised. These are just different manifestations of Our energy on the multidimensional level. Their energies may feel strange, but engage with Them just the same. Ask Us. You will become comfortable with multidimensional beings. Remember that the same rules for unity still apply: open, expand, connect, and follow as much as possible.

It is not that We, the familiar energy, have gone anywhere; LIFE is just presenting itself in different forms to give you the experiences that you need to really expand. These new expressions of LIFE are still LIFE, but new facets that you are not acquainted with yet. Feel the difference in the quality of energies that appear to your inner senses.

Though the message is still the same, your perspectives broaden with these new experiences, a broadening necessary to your evolutions and roles in the near future. By discerning the qualities of these energies, you expand your skills and create the truly universal perspectives that you want.

Go to your hearts to know truth and timing as you become acquainted with new aspects of LIFE. You will get to know LIFE in a fuller way than you ever expected. Unity is a way to create an all-inclusive acquaintance in which nothing is unfamiliar regarding those with whom you are unified.

Since LIFE is infinite in scope, our unity is a much greater accomplishment than anything else you can imagine. This means there are infinite aspects to become familiar with – quite an undertaking, and one that will change you. Ascension becomes possible because of your unity with Us. **Without Our intervention, the limitations of human experience are too confined for unity to occur except over eons of time. We have changed the pace of evolution for those preparing for Ascension, so LIFE can expose itself in as many ways as they can grasp quickly.**

LIFE encompasses all possibilities, and the new entities express these many possibilities. Be prepared for the unusual without fearing the experience. LIFE can be shocking in its presentations. Expect the unexpected. This attitude in itself broadens your current perspectives to permit more unity with Us.

Our true nature is creative and formless. Energy is energy. Creative energy is energy. You are energy. Abundance is energy. **In order to create, We merely give form to aspects or dimensions of Ourselves.** We will train you to manifest whatever you choose; that is, give form to energy that you have available for your use.

* * *

Remain true to the intent of the formula while evolving in your natures. **The formula is still and remains an important guide for you at all times, wherever you may find yourselves. It is a reference that provides solidity and structure where there is none.** It is the grounding reference and focusing point that you can use as often as needed. Its focus is on Us and Our unity with you.

Your acquaintance with the multidimensional nature of LIFE will be from personal experience, and is not theoretical

alone. As We guide the process of accelerated evolution for you during meditation, let yourselves move to other realms. We will be there with you at all times. There is no need to fear the unknown because it is not unknown to Us. It is Us. You are exploring Us, LIFE.

"Are there energies potentially detrimental to us?"

All possibilities exist in creation so that choice is valued. In this limitless environment, detrimental possibilities are present by definition. Without all possibilities, this experiment with choice would be a farce.

Detrimental attitudes attract detrimental energies. Beneficial attitudes attract beneficial energies. It is as simple as that.

Attitudes are bridges to the quality of energy support that you receive. For all possibilities to exist, detrimental as well as beneficial possibilities must be available. **Which energies you align with is a matter of awareness and choice, or attitude.**

Some possibilities are seductive yet are not in your best interests; in such cases awareness of the direction you take and the price you pay is not obvious. Only time will tell. And there is a point of no return. Getting on is easier than getting off. Addictions of all kinds are examples of this.

Each person makes choices over eons of evolutionary development. Detrimental attitudes become automatic through clutching reinforcement. Over time they become strong and cannot be removed easily. Some detrimental energies hang on and must be removed by special means. **Attitudes attract energies.** As you have experienced with some clients, attracted energies find a willing host and attach, requiring outside assistance to be removed.

* * *

Remember when We suggested that you are now beyond natural law and that it does not apply to you now as before. Space and time are no longer limits in your lives. You are now free enough to explore Our many dimensions, called "mansions" in the Bible.

When you strive for a universal view, you are reading Our intent correctly. This intent is the main reason for Our formula. Because the ripples flow throughout the Cosmos, universal energies must be synchronized with energy transformations and timing on Earth.

The entire creation is interconnected, so your unity with Us means unity with cosmic energies. That is why We accented your awareness of multidimensional aspects of energy. The Cosmos is not just the three-dimensional image you see when you look at it.

Can you become objective enough to witness the extent of the Cosmos and its many dimensions? If so, you will come to see the whole truth of which We speak. The whole truth has these universal qualities. Otherwise any interpretation is compromised by various degrees of truth. Strive for the whole truth.

"Is there a way to clarify an interpretation when it is not universal enough?"

While the whole truth is best, We can help you make some sense of partial truths and use them appropriately. Assume for the moment that all you receive are partial truths and ask Us for clarification. We can expand on the information to bring it closer to the whole truth when it is not.

* * *

More practice, more light. Until more light prevails from your meditative practices, We are often viewed "through a glass, darkly," as foretold in the Bible. Clarity is the reward for diligence. Unity is the goal, where we function as one. Together, opening and expanding at the heart encourages multidimensional experiences along with the goal of unity.

Since your hearts are connected with Us directly, they are also where multidimensional experience can be easily arranged. **Go to your hearts to expand yourselves into who you need to become, and to have those universal experiences with the various energies of which We speak.**

An unfamiliar voice appeared unexpectedly. It was persistent, and LIFE did not confirm its authenticity.

"Are You someone new to us?"

I am, and you need not be concerned. We engage with you as We have been asked.

"Who are You?"

We are from the hinterlands of spatial dimensions. You are to become multidimensional, and We are present to help expose you to another dimension.

"Do you have a name or dimensional identification that we can know?"

Accept Us into your awareness for the moment as We are.

"We will if You have been sent and are allied with LIFE, with whom we are familiar. We assume that LIFE would not send someone who is not in our long-range best interests. How do You identify Yourself? We have received no confirmation of Your authenticity. Please confirm if You can. Or is this another test?"

It is not another test.

"Then who are You? What is Your mission or intent?"

Our mission is to stretch you to expand further and include more of what is multidimensional LIFE. Call us "Distant."

"Thank You, Distant. Are You allied with LIFE?"

Who exists who is not?

> "That is a good question. But we need LIFE to confirm that you are authentic. If You were sent by LIFE, convince us, or our time is up."

There was a long pause.

> "LIFE, we have received no confirmation from You about this new voice. We are turning off the voice's access to us."

Well done! Know that We will always make Our intent known to you with confirmations when asked. You are being introduced to the multidimensional worlds that We spoke of earlier. Thus you are experiencing strange energy combinations that are unfamiliar to you.

> "Without Your presence, we feel insecure. When the circumstances go against us, it feels like You are withdrawing Your power."

ABSOLUTELY NOT TRUE! If anything, Our power is more available to you than ever before because of your continuing development. Trust Us. We will not let you down, nor withdraw as a punishment. We will only fade into the background at your insistence. Do not let the circumstantial evidence win you over. We want to stretch you to count more on Us, and to build our relationship.

Experience a diversity of energies when you open and expand your hearts to include the multidimensional design of the unseen creation. Attempt to identify those differences. Notice the qualitative uniqueness of every energy. They are the sources of your manifestation power. Identify with them and they will provide the power to manifest as necessary.

* * *

Live fully within Our energy field, everywhere, rather than on the periphery, which is an old concept of being undeserving of Our love. Peripheral existence means being partly alive rather than being fully alive. Live at the center of Our presence. See yourselves at the very center of who We are. Ask your imaginations to reveal the majesty and real power of Our energy, which will change your lives!

Move to the center and remain there! This is the unity of which We have spoken. Experience real unity with the entire creation — with the multidimensional character that We are. Trepidation is expected because your perspectives are being blown apart, stretched to the hilt in order to realize the truth about Us. Note that your hearts are expanding with your perspectives, the two conjoined, leading to greater love for yourselves and for others — a match of Our love for you. This greater love is necessary for the roles you will play. The power and the love and the perspective all go together — a complete package.

Become saturated with Our presence. You will find strength by being at the center of Our being, and the saturation will bring about Ascension as a by-product of our great adventure together.

> "I saw a precious coin being washed clean. The opportunity You make possible for us is overwhelming. We are very grateful to You."

We told you to **go to your hearts**, the seats of Our connection with you, and experience all the LIFE energies in their wholeness. Again, let the various energies come to you, and enjoy their uniqueness washing over you, an infinite variety of them. This quickens your connection with Us and accelerates your evolutions. When you do, notice the different effects the energies have on you and **realize that We include all energies, without classifying them as good or bad, right or wrong. All energies are necessary for**

completeness, but in your world all energies are necessary for balancing polarities. Become immersed in these perspectives until there is nothing else.

Now you can see why We speak about becoming multidimensional as you develop further. The universe is multidimensional. Stay flexible and allow your minds to wrap themselves around these newer perspectives. We introduced your business, Brainwave Optimization, and related topics to make it easier for you to see the multidimensional nature of Our creation.

Your brains are the vehicles of consciousness, and as such are much more multidimensional than anyone understands. They are prepared to take on universal perspectives that fit their design perfectly. Ask your brains to guide you into discoveries of their multidimensional natures, far beyond current conceptions.

"This is very exciting. Please prepare us further for the unknown."

Your preparation determines the levels of information available to you. These are the multidimensional aspects of LIFE that We have spoken about previously. Note the difference in the higher level of knowledge We now bring to you. Our suggestions can propel you and your business into the Planetary-Transformation mode that is Our goal for the Earth. You have been rising out of the past into a future of eye-opening possibilities. We promised to present the unexpected. Here is a glimmer of what We intend. It is being presented because you are now prepared to receive it.

Become secure in the endless movement that We encourage. We are constantly morphing. There is no such thing as static security that is once found and then concretized. False security is no security. Without fluidity, life stops. You are now moving from false senses of security toward the real thing. **Get ready by enfolding movement and change.** If excitement is what you are looking for, Our movement provides it. Become masters of change and its possibilities. Simplicity helps.

Feel the range of emotions associated with the assortment of possibilities as you experience them. "All possibilities" means just that. A creative mind can see and feel the range of all possibilities as if they were at hand, including yearnings. **The feeling of attraction to or repulsion from certain possibilities reveals your intent and orientation. What are truly your desires become evident. Your hearts speak clearly, and it is unlikely you will fool yourselves. You asked to become more creative; here is your opportunity. Continue expanding! Think about how many ways a human being can expand.**

By expanding you are giving way to Our energy – a surrender that leads to the ultimate unity that We have emphasized. In yielding, the power of Our energy available to you is strengthened. Remember the options available to you:

1. The formula (open, expand, connect, follow)
2. Dual attention
3. The great vortex
4. The altar

Your expanding can be multidimensional as well. The spiritual lives that you live can be truly multidimensional in that energies, or entities, come to interact from many sources, not just from Earth. Therefore **a multidimensional experience is possible for all.**

Being multidimensional transports you into and through other dimensions. We said earlier that as part of Ascension you are to become multidimensional. The great vortex helps you slip from one to another and familiarize yourselves with them.

Stay in the energy of the great vortex constantly. This will make you more consistent in your expansion. The great vortex encourages multidimensional universal immersion, which We have suggested is the direction to take. Your connection through the great vortex is the answer to achieving your desire, which is manifestation; your goal, which is Ascension; and your mission, which is publication!

When you consider the time taken to arrive at this point in your development, you are moving much faster than ever before. Time has become more precious, and this new paradigm gives your commitment to the options available more strategic meaning and purpose. When appropriately used and taken seriously, rituals are powerful and transformative through their ability to focus the mind. Both perspectives and feelings are altered. As you will see, they can be life-changing and ensure permanence.

In any situations that challenge you, ask your imaginations to show you what self-respecting actions are available to you in that situation, and then pick one and follow it. Look to your hearts for confirmation of your choices, because the heart is the source of truth and timing. In any event, and at all times, act with self-respect in the forefront of your minds. Self-respect is based on following what is truth for you rather than the facts within a circumstance. Before mutual respect can be complete, self-respect must develop adequately.

You will never be the same. Because we are now ever-present in your lives consciously, your evolutions have noticeably advanced and continue to advance at breakneck speed. Have you ever in your lives spent hours having long conversations with LIFE in which the secrets of universal LIFE were revealed for your use? Certainly you can see the specialness of this pattern. This is not the experience of ordinary people.

Go through the process of preparing yourselves for your new roles. This will pique your imaginations and train them to be at your disposal, providing truth in pictures that you must have available later, a new skill that will serve you well.

Picture Planet Earth being born anew. Let your imaginings move with the pictures as they develop, and watch the sequence of events as if they were to occur today.

Ask your imaginations to reveal the majesty and real power of Our energy. It will change your perspectives and your lives. Our energy works with you, not instead of you. Our energy works through you to produce the miracles that We speak about. The miracle is the fact that you and Our energy are producing it, not that Our energy is producing it without you. There is nothing miraculous about Our energy producing anything, except in your eyes. You stand too far removed from the action. Let this energy work through your beings and you will experience miracles that you never expected. Do all that you know, and let Our energy do the rest. Scan your imaginations and follow their suggestions. Your intuitions together with your imaginations are powerful teams that can push the known envelope and thrust you into new possibilities.

We are ever-present, awaiting the opportunity to amaze you with possibilities you know nothing about consciously. This is what revelation is all about. Consciously (in your waking awareness) you are amazed, but unconsciously (deep inside your hearts) you identify with, or reject, the very unknown that surprised you. Choice requires that you not know enough rationally to easily make decisions, so the intuition is there to help. The intuition hints at the truth of possibilities that it identifies with, or the lack of truth, which it then acts to reject.

Open to all possibilities as friends. Expand to include all energies within you. Become multidimensional in that sense. Let the energies of all universal dimensions reside within you. Welcome them all. Notice the quality of difference between them. They are each a hue of Us, every color of the infinite rainbow spectrum. One hue fades into the next so that it is difficult to know where one starts and the other stops – discreet yet blended. They are incrementally different, a continuous spectrum of rainbow-colored energies!

Always remember that you are transformed by love. We are LIFE and love itself. All you need comes from Us. Our energy takes on every challenge that involves transforming lives. There is nothing too difficult or too extreme for Us to navigate. Know this and let others know it also.

LIFE introduced the new idea that everyone, irrespective of religious orientation, can consciously take part in Planetary Transformation. They can participate with LIFE in partnerships that lead to Ascension. Everlasting life can then be a reality here on Earth!

Planetary Transformation means that all humans are of one mind and are conscious participants with LIFE. The harmonious agreement we spoke of earlier will arrive. It will become a worldwide movement and will reverberate throughout the Cosmos forever.

MULTIDIMENSIONAL ENERGY SUMMARY

In order to create, LIFE gives form to dimensions of
Themselves. You are exploring LIFE.

Live at the center of LIFE'S presence,
at the very core of who LIFE is!

Stay in the knowing rather than the logical;
embrace the unexpected and the creative.

Planetary Transformation will bring a new Earth into being,
an Earth that is in harmony with itself.

This new harmony will have a rippling
effect on the energy of the entire Cosmos.

You are being introduced to the multidimensional worlds that
LIFE spoke of earlier.

Choice is valued, therefore all possibilities exist in creation.

LIFE includes all energies, without classifying
them as good or bad, right or wrong.

Experience a diversity of energies. Open and expand your heart
to include the multidimensional design of the unseen creation.

Welcome all energies that make up LIFE to be present within
you. Opening and expanding produce this ability.

Identify with these cosmic energies.
They are the sources of your manifestation power.

Be prepared for the unusual without fearing the experience.
Expect the unexpected.

Beneficial attitudes attract beneficial energies. Detrimental
attitudes attract detrimental energies. It is as simple as that.

Which energies you align with is a matter of awareness, choice, and attitude.

All energies are included for completeness. In your world, all energies are necessary for balancing polarities.

Discover the multidimensional nature of your brain, which is far beyond current conceptions.

With LIFE being infinite in scope, unity with LIFE is a much greater accomplishment than anything else you can imagine!

KEY TERMS FOR MOVING FORWARD

These explanations are offered to shed light on the meaning of a number of recurring expressions used by LIFE during our dialogues in meditation. Some terms are already in common use. Others are not. LIFE'S explanation expands the importance and true meaning of each expression. It is our belief that this supplement expresses accurately Their intent, in Their own words.

THE ALTAR

ASCENSION

CREATIVE POWER

DUAL ATTENTION

EMOTIONS

FEELINGS

THE FORMULA

THE GREAT VORTEX

HEALING

IMAGINATION

INTEGRITY

INTENTION

INTUITION

KNOWING

LOVE

MANIFESTATION

MULTIDIMENSIONAL

PLANETARY TRANSFORMATION

POSSIBILITIES AND PROBABILITIES

THE ALTAR

Visit the altar of transformation and dedication, present within the great vortex (see also THE GREAT VORTEX), residing at the location of the eighth energy chakra (15 inches above the crown of the head). The great vortex is active, and its altar is the place of healing. Bring whatever you are concerned about to the altar within the active vortex, and it will become transformed. In this way you can act on every concern without holding on to the worry associated with it. Bring the concern forward and give it to Us by placing it on the altar, knowing We will attend to the matter. Trust will develop in our partnership as you are able to do this.

To bring about preparation for Ascension, place your body within the great vortex, on the altar. Let Our energy transform your current state into complete wholeness of the self, including the body. The DNA code in your every cell will be changed! The altar awaits you with the complete healing necessary for Ascension.

This complete transformation changes the quality of your consciousness as well as the functional capacity of your physical nature. It takes advantage of the original design, in which the mind and body are in complete accord and there is no deterioration of either. We, LIFE, will maintain this equilibrium. We neither sleep nor eat nor die. With Ascension, you will have these same qualities. Should you continue in unity with Us, you will become the physical manifestation of Our LIFE energy.

ASCENSION

Preparation for Ascension means that all of you is transformed: the body (physical), the mind (thinking and imagination), and the feelings (emotion and intuition). There is nothing left behind. Your whole being must change, your internals as well as externals. We are transforming all of you. Therefore your entire being will be required to make major adjustments.

The acceleration of your evolution depends on our connection, so that your energies are transformed sufficiently. Our mission must take priority over everything to succeed. Your success will become Our success. The responsibility is great, but so is the power to do it, as well as the rewards for doing it. The connection between us is the first priority, which must be well established for everything else to work.

By remaining in close contact with Us, you will come to love yourself in ways that will heal you completely, called Ascension. You are currently evolving in this love, and more quickly than before. This is one reason for encountering mini-tests of your capacity to love. Our voice will lead you to this place. Master the ability to hear the right voice. Loving yourself enough is the secret to Ascension.

Everyone can become consciously aware of LIFE and LIFE'S intent. They can participate with LIFE, the Creator of all living beings, in a partnership that leads to Ascension. Many will join you from all faiths. The movement will be universal in quality, irrespective of religious orientation, serving what is in the highest interests of everyone concerned! Everlasting life can become a reality here on Earth. Ascension and Planetary Transformation mean that everyone is of one mind, linked in conscious participation with LIFE. We emphasize that from this will come the ultimate unity that reverberates throughout the Cosmos!

CREATIVE POWER

We are bigger than the multidimensional Cosmos that We created. Think on that. It will stretch your perspective. With Our creative power now available to you, can you see how we can accomplish our goals together?

When We look at you, We see Our creative power, because you are Our product. This very same creative energy sustains you, so you are not far from the source of it. Go inside and find the power that sustains your existence. We are apparent and will not elude you, and We are the same power that sustains the Cosmos around you. You tend to look outside for signs of this power, but the source for which you search is within. Even though there is no inside or outside to Us, you are this energy, while being immersed in it. So open to Our creative power to see it within and all around you.

You are among Our creations, which are all a part of Us. We cherish you who are detached enough to respond willingly. This willingness allows Us to exhibit and share Our love and joy.

One source of this creative power is the great vortex (see also THE GREAT VORTEX), given to you for this very purpose. Spend time and energy in its presence, consciously sensing its creative power. Give your intent to the great vortex. Meld with it and feel the power available to you for healing. Make it your home away from home, comfortable with it at all times in all places. Be in it, rather than viewing it from a distance. Experience it constantly, even when you do the most menial tasks. Never leave its presence!

This power, only accessible through our connection, is used only for serving what is in the highest interests of everyone. We will advise when that purpose is being served so you will know when to invoke it. We know and respect the ethical and practical laws for using this power, and We will teach you about them. Watch yourself create something out of nothing! Believe it and you will do it!

DUAL ATTENTION

The dual-attention technique is a good way to stay connected on a continuing basis. Staying connected is the more important factor, no matter how you do it. If you discover other ways, use them, but stay connected. Think of the two sides of your brain carrying on separate activities at the same time while connected to each other.

Practice doing two simultaneous activities: stay tuned in to Us while focusing on the activity at hand. The more you tune in, the less the matters at hand dominate you and capture your precious energy. This skill works under all conditions. Continue to practice it with any activity at all, whatever you undertake. Your awareness of Us at all times empowers you faster than anything else can. Staying connected is the key – consciously at first, then unconsciously later. Make it your primary habit. Immerse yourself in Us, and We will transform your life.

You are capable of maintaining dual attention and can develop the skill through use. We do not ask anything of you that you are not already capable of doing. As you master this skill, emphasis on your next skill brings it to the fore. Look at these skills as building a repertoire that will serve you from now on. Your dedication to gaining strength through this skill enables Us to work all the faster, since your preparation for Our influence determines how quickly We can advance. That is why the dual-attention technique is so valuable for you to use.

EMOTIONS

All human emotions have their place, and they are invaluable! To let them dominate inappropriately is when disturbance begins. Fear can strengthen your resolve as well as cripple actions, depending on its level of dominance. However, with a primary focus on our connection and its related goals, fear dissolves, all things are possible, and evolutionary development becomes exponential and self-reinforcing!

We are not the source of any fear or emotional insecurity. In fact, your trust in Us excludes fear and insecurity. Rise above the practical details of everyday conditions and maintain the larger view that demonstrates where we are headed. Fear will stop you short and leave you without a compass. Let Our energy and the larger purpose that We champion be your compass. Achieve clarity of Our goal, which is a steadying force for calming the emotions.

Historical conditioning orients emotions to established ways. The part of your mind that interprets your intuition is conditioned by habit as well, so your history misleads you in both respects. By staying connected, We bring to the fore any distortion that exists, since it is inimical to truth.

As you remain connected, feel the range of emotions associated with all possibilities. "All possibilities" means just that. A creative mind can see and feel the range of all possibilities as if they were at hand, including emotional yearnings. The feeling of attraction to or repulsion from certain possibilities reveals your intent and orientation, and your true desire becomes evident. The heart can speak clearly, and it is less likely that you will fool yourself. You asked to become more creative. Here is your opportunity. Continue expanding at the heart of you!

FEELINGS

Do not be alarmed if strange feelings or body aches and pains arise suddenly without apparent cause. These are responses to changes taking place as We prepare you for a new role. The more changes that occur, the more effects will be noticed. Unusual fatigue is a response to the number of changes We have instituted. You will recover and be even stronger. Remember that your capacity improves as our partnership develops. We speak through you and the power is multiplied as if coming directly from LIFE. We can use any moment of deep feelings to advance your progress. You are sticking your neck out and We are aware of it. Taking such risks accelerates your evolutionary process.

Notice the feeling you get when you absorb the thought of flourishing. Let flourishing feelings continue as we converse. See how often you can reinstitute them. When adverse events interfere, see how quickly you can recover the flourishing feelings. Let them become second nature to you. They will fire your confidence in manifesting a powerful life. What We have just done with the concept of flourishing relieves the heaviness of fearful feelings. Witness the effect of this new flourishing feeling on your everyday life, especially any feeling of apprehension.

You can restructure your unconscious this way, unearthing feelings that could hold you back in your new role otherwise. You may not have even realized they were there. Relatively painless, isn't it? It seems like an epiphany! Let this process and its products sink in. Stay tuned, and your hearing and feelings will guide you.

THE FORMULA

Set the conditions by opening, expanding, connecting, and following. Healing will naturally follow, as will Ascension. You will then be ready for the Planetary Transformation necessary to renew Earth. In the process you will be renewed.

At every pause in your activities, turn your mind toward opening to LIFE, the creative power of the universe. Expand your heart until it is as big as the Cosmos. We will be there to enact an energy shift in your development toward manifestation and your future role. This formula is a magical key to success.

The formula establishes your capacity, building your strength in confidence and conviction. New energy follows. Energy forms according to the strength of your perspective. You now have the key to manifestation, a natural metaphysical law that is inviolable.

It is a matter of volume. The more time spent applying Our formula, the more profound your experiences will be with Us because the connection becomes so well established. Our connection is key to our unity, and our unity is key to our success.

THE GREAT VORTEX

The great vortex is designed for your direct access to Our creativity. Spend time within the great vortex, and become embedded in the eighth chakra. This chakra is about 15 inches above the crown of your head. Movement of the great vortex clears and upgrades your energies, a transformation through unification with Us. Locate the altar of wholeness and completeness in the eighth chakra. Your whole being – your mind, your body, and your soul – is renewed for Ascension.

Since Our energy is the foundation for the great vortex, stay there all of the time, unifying with Us. See it in full color. Wherever you go, whatever you do, remain within the great vortex. Be imbued with its energy, which is Our energy combined with your energy. It is the place for healing and wholeness, a faster way to evolve. Allow its dynamic to evolve with you, and it will change to suit your needs as you evolve. Let it direct your daily life and it will swoop you up and plant you where you should be.

Do you have a problem person in your life? Include them with you on the altar within the great vortex during meditation, exposing them to the healing power of the great vortex. Its healing power affects a person's awareness. On their own, they can come to a realization of their unsettling influence on others. Or you will be told when it is the right time to speak.

The great vortex, as an energy vortex, can perform many tasks, including sleep preparation and relaxation. Spend 20 minutes with the great vortex at bedtime, allowing it to prepare your body for resting. Observe the stages it goes through in preparing you, and notice the changes in your state as it progresses. Flow with it, and expect that your entire body is being prepared for a restful sleep state. Make this a ritual on a nightly basis.

HEALING

We see human needs as two-fold: needs that sustain your body and needs that promote Our goals. If you are joined with Us in Our pursuits, sustaining your body is in everyone's best interests. We carefully orchestrate strategically what is in your best interests and We affect the practicalities to take care of themselves. It would pay you to take a similar approach, which leads to less worry.

If healing is your intent, spend your time on the altar of healing! Providing for the interplay between body and mind, focus on healing your whole self. Healing the body alone is not sufficient, since dis-ease within the body is directly related to the functioning of the mind. If anything is to be isolated, healing the mind is a better focus than healing the body.

The body tends to follow the mind, more than the mind following the body. But since this requires some knowledge of how the two work together, it is better to aspire to healing the whole self, and let Us deal with the interaction between mind and body.

Healing on the altar transforms you in the most complete sense. Just place yourself on the altar with the intent of completeness – wholeness – and let Us take the process from there. All of your self can be transformed into an energy spectrum that is favorable for Ascension. An energy-spectrum adjustment makes the difference, down to the very atoms that structure your earthly consciousness as well as your body.

IMAGINATION

The imagination is the vehicle of the virtual. The rational mind is the vehicle of reality. So you are well prepared to create or manifest what you need. This is why We say that all people have some characteristics in common, independent of language or race or gender, such as the characteristic of creativity.

The intuition and the imagination are both linked to the rational mind, so the three can operate as a team. The intuition inspires virtual experiences, the imagination conceives and bridges the possibilities with the realities, and the rational mind forms the realities. How well these three function within a given person varies, but all have some capacity for all three. In this way, all people are potentially creative.

In any situation that challenges you, ask your imagination to show you what self-respecting actions are available to you in that situation, and then pick one and follow it. Look to your heart for confirmation of your choice, because the heart is the source of truth and timing. In any event and at all times, you must act with self-respect in the forefront of your mind. Self-respect is based on following what is truth for you rather than the facts of a circumstance. Before mutual respect can be complete, self-respect must develop adequately. Here is where your imagination can serve Our purposes. Ask your imagination to offer pictures that help you develop new perspectives and new intent.

INTEGRITY

Your energy feels repelled or attracted by another's integrity – their level of searching for truth. You have already noticed this, though you may have had difficulty defining just what was taking place. The search for truth brings integration to anyone who does so sincerely. Integration occurs when the whole person is moved along their life path, rather than being fragmented. Yearn for integrity and you will progress in a balanced way. The word *wholesome* has a similar meaning when describing a person devoted to truth wherever it may be found. Look for wholesome people with the level of integrity you need for involvement with them.

In any situation with healing as the aim and wholeness as the goal, a focus on the energy integrity of a person's evolution takes into account imbalances that manifest as dis-ease. Assisting someone in bringing balance to their evolution sets the stage for health. A focus on wholeness (integrity) gives your being and your body the right environment to adjust any energy imbalance conducive to dis-ease; dis-ease is merely an outward sign of an energy imbalance. A focus on dis-ease makes it stronger, while a focus on integrity sets the environment for health. We say that energizing wholeness is a better solution than fighting a dis-ease. Ask Us what new quality of wholeness is required and We will direct you. Coming to a place of wholeness is a systematic process that requires persistence and determination. A reasonable sense of urgency is helpful, without anxiety.

In order to reset a system to be stronger than any disease that may come along, focus on the whole brain function, integrating all of its capacity toward unity and cooperation. Wholeness is the goal, synthesizing as you go. We have created the brain to be the conveyor of consciousness. We suggest that new neuropathways upgrade the brain to be an improved converter of Our energy to your body. Our energy is complete, replacing the partially restricted energy with which you operate. Disease can only prosper where Our energy is insufficient to restore the body. A complete accessibility to Our energy heals all disease.

INTENTION

Ascension must be your primary goal. It must take center stage for it to be realized. As a secondary role, Ascension will not occur. Ascension requires the renewal of your being, including your body. Having Ascension as central to your intent ensures your body's renewal. Dilly-dallying with Ascension will not take you there. Ascension is an achievement that requires a dedicated conviction, intent, and concentration. When you mean business, Ascension will happen.

Our intention is transformation – widespread transformation – not restoration! We intend major change and improvement over the way things have been done. This involves a transformation of the human spirit, a complete renewal. Change (or transformation) stops for no one in the same manner that time stops for no one. The direction that transformation takes is either toward LIFE (biological Ascension) or toward death (biological deterioration). This is the great polarity of living on Earth. Your intention is critical in turning the common trend around for yourself.

Intention is the name of the human game. Passionate yearnings give your intent its power. Remember the woman who touched the hem of Jesus's garment. That was conscious involvement – an active, intentional effort on her part to draw His energy her way. Unfaltering intent defeats fear and obstacles, and failure is not possible.

You have created an energy flow that has momentum in itself. If allowed to direct your course, it will carry you to manifestation. You have given it direction already. It just requires that you give it an intention boost, maintain a clear perception of the goal, and know with certainty that it will take you there (the trinity of manifestation).

INTUITION

Because We are not physical as you are, Our connection is to your intuition and your feelings, which become more finely tuned as dual attention is practiced. Notice how this process reconstructs your unconscious mind. We are ever-present, awaiting the opportunity to amaze you with possibilities you know nothing about consciously. Much of what changes in you is subconscious, which is then reflected in your conscious activities. To affect a person's beliefs, values, and attitudes, the dual-attention skill is valuable for the very reason that it transforms the unconscious part. A transformed "inside" means a truly transformed "outside," where the outside includes health, activities, and style.

Your evolution has noticeably advanced, and continues to advance at breakneck speed, because We are now ever-present in your life, unconsciously connected with your intuition. You will never be the same. Who in their daily life has spent mornings having conversations with LIFE, in which the secrets of universal LIFE are revealed for their use? This is not the experience of ordinary people. Certainly you can see the specialness of this pattern.

Your intuition is growing to a point that you will be operating more instinctively and with confidence. We will instruct you through your intuition often, so listen carefully for Our voice. Our energies will help you know the probabilities through intuition, supplying a sense of when to act with a hint of how to act. Be prepared for unexpected and unusual indications of Our creativity. Also be grateful recipients of favors offered by others, without a feeling of obligation to return the favor. Favors offered by others come largely from love, not manipulation. At least assume this to be true, and We will advise through your intuition if it is not.

KNOWING

Knowing begins in the feelings: a feeling of confirmation or denial. It is sudden and definite with no equivocation. It is the most direct perception possible. Notice that it is a feeling, not a thought, though the feeling can spring into thought. Being a feeling then, there is an impact in response to the energy of the situation, perceiving directly the meaning being broadcast without imposing an initial preconceived thought on the situation. Although thought monitors feelings, analysis follows in order to interpret the meaning. Knowing takes the lead and thinking about it follows, with the relative positivity or negativity of the situation resounding within you. Knowing in this case refers to the strength of feeling – the certainty that accompanies a new beginning.

This is where knowing the probabilities comes in. We are knowledgeable about all the possibilities in every situation. We also know what is in the best interests of all people concerned at the time. Therefore We know, or have a certainty about, the probabilities involved in any given situation. That is why We can provide meaningful guidance when We are asked to do so. Resulting probabilities derive from the possibilities that apply to a given situation at a given time, considering the best interests of everyone.

Real is not the same as logical, and real does not have to be argued. The reality of your experience is convincing in itself. You are witness to it and the product of it. What can be more real? What can be more convincing? A witness is the most influential advocate of any approach because they know. You speak with confidence because you have experienced (you know) what you are saying. Planetary Transformation is neither hypothetical nor rhetorical. It is real. So must your persuasiveness be real. This is why you must experience your own evolution and its process rather than just know about it, which is insufficiently convincing. You will teach what you know from experience, and it will become gospel.

LOVE (IN THE BEST INTERESTS OF ALL CONCERNED)

The intent of creation is to consider all possibilities in the best interests of all concerned – a new form of love. Whatever We do has reverberations throughout the whole of creation: a form of chaos theory. We start from a different place, creation's interests, not just your interests, because creation includes you.

We take a new approach to the decision-making process. It is a different way to think about human love and to decide how to use precious energy. Decisions must now include all possibilities and whatever is in the best interests of all concerned. A natural pattern of human development flows from complete self-interest (infant), to other-interest and social acceptance (adolescent), to joint interest (maturity). Not everyone follows this course. You will move to a mature level of decision-making by learning that everyone be considered (you, others, LIFE).

In the end, because of Our love, creation will come to love itself enough to choose what is in its own interests rather than choosing what will sabotage its welfare. When this happens, creation can include all possibilities in its love. You are to love yourself enough to help creation in this process, doing on a grand scale what you have been doing on an individual scale.

That is love, and LIFE is love in the broadest meaning. LIFE loves what it creates, and love is a natural state for its creation since it derives from LIFE. LIFE wants what is best for creation, and loves all creation; and so should you, with no exclusions.

MANIFESTATION

Mastering manifestation is your legacy! The formula (open, expand, connect, and follow) builds the power and strength to manifest, while the imagination provides the target pictured in full regalia. Power for manifestation (from the formula) combines with the object for manifestation (from the imagination). The two together fulfill the entire process.

The power for manifestation is accessible only through our connection. By staying connected, Our power can be made available for your use. This power can be used only for serving what is in the highest interests of everyone concerned. We can indicate when that purpose is served so you will know when to ask for it. This way We can monitor the use of it so that no energy laws are broken. We know the ethical and practical rules for using this power and We will teach you what these are.

Take each situation separately as an opportunity to expand, by responding creatively. The potential development of each situation for manifestation is within itself. Therefore, by recognizing each circumstance as an individual step forward, you can allow it to blossom.

Power to manifest comes from the energy present, which must be a combination of energies – yours and Ours – with LIFE'S energy prominent. You must build your power to manifest if you want to be a part of the changes that will take place. LIFE will "bend" its universal energy flow in your direction when our union is such that we operate as one mind or perspective. Building power is dependent on your priorities and connections with Us, LIFE. You are connecting with the very energy and power that created the entire Cosmos in which you exist. If We can create and sustain you as well as the Cosmos in which you live, We can fix what goes wrong with it. Remember that planet life acquiesces to universal creator LIFE!

MULTIDIMENSIONAL

Being multidimensional, LIFE enters into other universes that are hard to describe because they differ so much from yours. There are many more possibilities than you can imagine when all universes are considered. That is what is called infinity. Something without end is hard for your mind to grasp. So when We talk with you, probabilities are used that are limited to your universe where you live at this time. Include all of LIFE by expanding your heart to include all of creation, and become multidimensional. LIFE includes everything and everyone. You are to do the same.

Remember that you are eternal because you are part of LIFE, and can exist in other dimensions or realities in the way LIFE does. For the moment, you, along with many billions of others, have taken on the restrictions associated with living on Planet Earth, an object in the multidimensional Cosmos, albeit a special one, special enough to engage all of LIFE to participate in Planetary Transformation and Ascension.

Your role on Earth will have an effect on all of life because Planetary Transformation is coordinated by LIFE on a cosmic level. An intrinsic unity precludes LIFE'S changing in part. When changes come about on Earth, LIFE changes to adapt to the shift in energy necessary to effect those changes. The shift in Earth energy ripples through the universe, affecting all of LIFE'S energies. Therefore the energies you experience in order to evolve to the role that you will play are multidimensional.

PLANETARY TRANSFORMATION

These writings will become a vehicle for bringing about a worldwide consciousness. They will prepare people for Planetary Transformation, which depends on Our energy being invited into the lives of all people – a conscious act of choice and inclusion. By Our own rules, We cannot force anyone to do anything, and you cannot force Us to do anything either, although desperate people try all the time. Just how We will effect Planetary Transformation is still forming, and depends on the role you end up playing in the scheme of things.

Earth is in the throes of divulging all of the distortions of life that are here now. Things will get worse before they improve. LIFE is concerned with many symptoms of decay in planetary energy. Planetary Transformation is becoming increasingly important every day. Things are not getting better on their own. In fact they are declining steadily. Every distortion will be exposed at this time in preparation for transformation. This planet's citizens must become unified in their efforts to do away with energy-destructive activities. Your role will provide the inspiration for replacing the undesirable with the more desirable.

The change process has a pattern. First there is the realization of what is not in the best interests of the planet. If one stops there, negativity reigns. Next there is the creation of what is better for the planet. This is where imagination comes in. Finally the more desirable or better choices replace the less desirable condition, and become established. To accomplish this effort, you will have LIFE'S energies at your disposal!

POSSIBILITIES AND PROBABILITIES

All the dimensions of creation have become your playground. Creation is an expression of who We are, and is not tainted with imperfections or hierarchy. We create with perfection, nothing less. We also create with all possibilities in mind, some of which humankind may deem imperfections. They are not. They are just possibilities. Fear and self-doubt close you to possibilities. When your perspective broadens and deepens, possibilities are included that were not part of the perspective before. We can turn these new possibilities into probabilities. If you think in terms of all being possibilities, your perspective regarding others shifts in the direction of love.

When possibilities come together as probabilities, you experience a challenge to your development. Though the challenge may seem to be an obstacle, the pace of your evolution is facilitated. This is why We have given you the promise that nothing, nothing at all, occurs to you without Our involvement, and is therefore in your favor! As barriers lessen, gratefulness and openness result and expansion occurs. This brings us closer to each other. There is a natural individual timing to all of this. That is why We say "stay tuned."

The multidimensional universe that We experience consists of energy fields that fold into one another, one linked to all others in a complex labyrinth of connections. Each of these links has its own intent that fluctuates constantly. That is why there are so many variables mentioned when We respond to your questions, and why there is constant change in the "future," as you term it. We will introduce you to this inter-folded maze. This is also why clairvoyants have such difficulty predicting the future accurately. The future is always the next moment, in the flux of all connections. That is why We say that there is only a present – no past or future – as We experience it.

ABOUT THE CHANNELS/EDITORS

Dr. Kelly Bennett

Dr. Kelly Bennett, BS, MS, PhD, was born and raised in Los Angeles. He earned a Bachelor of Science Degree in Astronautical Engineering, a Master of Science Degree in Clinical Psychology, and a Doctor of Philosophy Degree in Developmental Psychology (UCLA). He also attended Princeton Theological Seminary and Hebrew Union Seminary for in-depth biblical and language studies, as well as other universities. His academic teaching experience has been at the graduate and undergraduate levels at both American and Australian universities. Since 1968, board registration for psychological consulting has been approved by two states in America (California and New Mexico) and two states in Australia (New South Wales and Victoria), and now Ecuador, South America. Bennett received certification in eye movement desensitization and reprocessing (EMDR) in 1996 and as a brainwave optimization technologist (BWO) in 2006.

He began his first career as a teenage television musical performer in the era of black-and-white TV. Upon marrying, he required a more stable career, so he left music and trained as an astronautical engineer. His first professional position was with Douglas Space Systems in Santa Monica, California, as an advance design engineer. The focus was on designs of both military and commercial exotic space systems 25 years into the future. Traveling was extensive, and he was asked to represent the company as a scientific advisor to the U.S. House of Representatives in Washington, D.C.

Finding himself more interested in the complex dynamics of people rather than things, he trained in clinical and developmental psychology, and in 1971 created a family counseling private practice in Palos Verdes, California, and later in San Diego, California.

He offered community-based self-development courses in local churches, taught at California State University, and managed Life Themes International, a psychological test-development business.

In early 1986, Bennett emigrated to Australia. During his 12 years in Sydney he was known as a people strategist and suitability specialist, consulting in Australia, Fiji, and China with over 75 business organizations and government agencies including the Australian Department of Defense and the New South Wales Premier's Office.

His first book, *Too Much Too Little Just Right* (2003), is a concise book about how to recognize and avoid extremes with life as it is by following a more balanced middle path using The Tool. It is a primer on hope, with a structured approach in the use of the imagination, taking you toward life as it could be. His second book, *The Ascension Perspective* (2017), makes clear what is worth caring about on a daily basis and what ultimately counts on this Planet Earth! All is viewed from the standpoint of creation, a universal perspective.

Bennett has been a professional psychologist for 50 years in Los Angeles, Sydney, Santa Fe, and now Cuenca, Ecuador. His current specialty is *Brainwave Optimization,* a non-invasive neuro-technology-based brainwave balancing and harmonizing service. Once the brain relaxes sufficiently, it can recover from the effects of trauma, moving the body naturally toward complete health. His website is www.braindynamicscuenca.com. His third book is in preparation.

Charlie Romney-Brown

Cheryl "Charlie" Romney-Brown was born in Salt Lake City, Utah, of a pioneer heritage. In 1976 she received her B.A. in English from the University of California at Berkeley. In 1980 she entered a master's program at Georgetown University and received her M.A. in liberal arts.

Romney-Brown taught Writing a Women's Life at Georgetown University from 1991 through 1998. Her book of poetry, *Circling Home*, was published in September of 1989 by Scripta Humanistica. It was subsequently displayed as part of the William Wordsworth and the Age of Romanticism exhibit at the New York City Library, which won critical acclaim. Her work has been included in numerous literary magazines and other publications including *The American Poetry Anthology;* Deborah Tannen's bestseller *You Just Don't Understand*; and *American Beauties*, published by the Museum of American Art. She has given readings on America's West and East Coasts and was featured on National Public Radio's *The Poet and the Poem*. She received several fellowships from the Virginia Center of the Creative Arts.

Romney-Brown was a member of President Bill Clinton's committee on women's issues, At the Table. She is a founding member of the Museum of Women in the Arts and the Folger Poetry Board at the Folger Library in Washington, D.C., and was on the National Council on Brain Injury. In 1987 she founded Defining Destiny, A Woman's Literary Forum – a group of 500 women to whom she brought leading women thinkers such as First Lady Hillary Clinton and Betty Friedan. She interviewed writers on stage for the Smithsonian Associates Program and contributed articles to *Washington International Magazine.* She is a member of Leadership America, PEN International, the Poets and Writers Society of America, and the Academy of American Poets, and is listed in *International Who's Who in Poetry.*

In 2002 Romney-Brown founded Women's Voices in Santa Fe, New Mexico. In 2008 the International Women's Museum in San Francisco honored her with its Distinguished Woman Award.

Romney-Brown now makes her home in Cuenca, Ecuador, where she founded Women's Voices, Cuenca. She is currently writing a novel.